Advanced Educational Technology

Published by:
Saurabh Publishing House

Advanced Educational Technology

C.P. Singh

Saurabh
Publishing House
4735/22, Prakash Deep Building,
Ansari Road, Daryaganj,
New Delhi- 110002

Published by :
SAURABH PUBLISHING HOUSE

Distributed by :
Lotus Press Publishers & Distributors
Unit No. 220, 2nd Floor, 4735/22, Prakash Deep Building,
Ansari Road, Darya Ganj, New Delhi- 110002
Ph.: 41325510, 09811838000
• E-mail : lotuspress1984@gmail.com
www.lotuspress.co.in

Saurabh Publishing House is an imprint of
Lotus Press Publishers & Distributors

Advanced Educational Technology

ISBN: 978-81-89005-79-5

Printed by : **Lotus Press Publishers & Distributors, New Delhi**

Preface

Educational technology research always had an ambitious agenda. Sometimes, it only aims at increased efficiency or effectiveness of current practise, but frequently, it aims at pedagogical change. While it can be considered as a design science, it also addresses fundamental issues of learning, teaching and social organization and therefore makes use of the full range of modern social science and life sciences methodology.

"Technology provides us with powerful tools to try out different designs, so that instead of theories of education, we may begin to develop a science of education. But it cannot be an analytic science like physics or psychology; rather it must be a design science more like aeronautics or artificial intelligence. For example, in aeronautics the goal is to elucidate how different designs contribute to lift, drag maneuverability, etc. Similarly, a design science of education must determine how different designs of learning environments contribute to learning, cooperation, motivation, etc."

Technology is therefore both a tool and a catalyzer and it can become a medium through which change can happen.

Educational technologists would not therefore consider the computer as just another piece of equipment. If educational technology is concerned with thinking carefully about teaching and learning, then a computer has a contribution to make irrespective of its use as a means of implementation, for the design of computer-based learning environments gives us a new perspective on the nature of teaching and learning and indeed on general educational objectives.

The major topics dealt in this book are: *Educational Technology; Instructional Design and Technology; E-Learning; Learning Management System; Microlearning; Multimedia Learning; Applied Behavior Analysis; Virtual Learning Environment; Virtual University; Educational Software; Computer and Digital Technology; Educational Assessment; Glossary of Education;* etc.

We express our gratitude to various scholars, teachers and friends for their assistance and guidance. Finally, we thank our publisher for bringing out this book in very limited time.

–*Author*

Contents

1
Educational Technology

Educational technology is a wide field. Therefore, one can find many definitions, some of which are conflicting. Educational technology can be considered either as a design science or as a collection of different research interests addressing fundamental issues of learning, teaching and social organization. Nevertheless, there are a few features on which most researchers and practitioners might agree:

1. Use of technology is principled: Technology means the systematic application of scientific knowledge to practical tasks. Therefore, educational technology is based on theoretical knowledge drawn from different disciplines (communication, education, psychology, sociology, philosophy, artificial intelligence, computer science, etc.) plus experiential knowledge drawn from educational practice.

2. Educational technology aims to improve education. Technology should facilitate learning processes and increase performance of the educational system(s) as it regards to effectiveness and/or efficiency.

In this short introduction, we will try to give a preliminary definition of the field.

Other Definitions

Educational technology is a very wide field. Therefore one can find many definitions, some of which are conflicting.

- Technology means the systematic application of scientific or other organized knowledge to practical task. Therefore, educational technology is based on theoretical knowledge from different disciplines (communication, psychology, sociology, philosophy, artificial intelligence, computer science, etc.) plus experiential knowledge from educational practise.

- The study and ethical practice of facilitating learning and improving performance by creating, using and managing appropriate technological processes and resources.

- Educational technology is the use of technology to improve education. It is a systematic, iterative process for designing instruction or training used to improve performance. Educational technology is sometimes also known as instructional technology or learning technology.

- "One definition of Educational Technology is that it is a systematic, iterative process for designing instruction or training used to improve performance"

- A definition centred on its process: "A complex, integrated process involving people, procedures, ideas, devices, and organization, for analyzing problems, and devising, implementing, evaluating and managing solutions to those problems, involved in all aspects of human learning".

- Lachance *et al.* also focus on the the process idea: la technologie educative en tant que processus systematique integrant les diverses fonctions du processus educatif. Elle vise, d'une part, a analyser des problemes relies a l'enseignement et/ou a l'apprentissage et, d'autre part, a elaborer, implanter et evaluer des solutions a ces problèmes par le developpement et l'exploitation des ressources educatives.

- Educational Technology (Information Technology) according to International Technology Education Association
    1. Teaches with technology (uses technology as a tool).
    2. Primarily concerned with the narrow spectrum of information and communication technologies.
    3. Primary goal: To enhance the teaching and learning process.

Terminology issue: Educational technology is a field. A educational technology refers to a technology that is particularly suited for education plus its usage/range of applications maybe. See the educational technologies article and the category educational technologies.

Goals of Educational Technology

Educational technology research always had an ambitious agenda. Sometimes it only aims at increased efficiency or effectiveness of current practise, but frequently it aims at pedagogical change. While it can be considered as a design science it also addresses fundamental issues of learning, teaching and social organization and therefore makes use of the full range of modern social science and life sciences methodology.

> "Technology provides us with powerful tools to try out different designs, so that instead of theories of education, we may begin to develop a science of education. But it cannot be an analytic science like physics or psychology; rather it must be a design science more like aeronautics or artificial intelligence. For example, in aeronautics the goal is to elucidate how different designs contribute to lift, drag maneuverability, etc. Similarly, a design science of education must determine how different designs of

learning environments contribute to learning, cooperation, motivation, etc."

Technology is therefore both a tool and a catalyzer and it can become a medium through which change can happen.

Educational technologists would not therefore consider the computer as just another piece of equipment. If educational technology is concerned with thinking carefully about teaching and learning, then a computer has a contribution to make irrespective of its use as a means of implementation, for the design of computer-based learning environments gives us a new perspective on the nature of teaching and learning and indeed on general educational objectives.

Defining the field is both simple (e.g., see the definitions at the top) and difficult. There are several perspectives.

From an Instructional Design Perspective

Besides being a field of research, Educational Technology is synonymous for { Pedagogy, Learning, Instructional design, etc.} with technology and therefore also an engineering discipline, a design science or an craft (whatever you prefer).

In order to define educational technology we may ask ourselves what constitutes an instructional design and what disciplines look at these constituents.

Even from a pure "engineering perspective," it doesn't make much sense to talk about Educational Technology just in terms of Instructional design models or instructional design methods. An instructional designer also feels concerned by more fundamental disciplines like general learning theory or pedagogical theory. These theories provide interesting insights on issues like the relation between learning type or learning level and appropriate pedagogic strategy, how affect and motivation may influence the learning process, what multimedia design can learn from theories on human

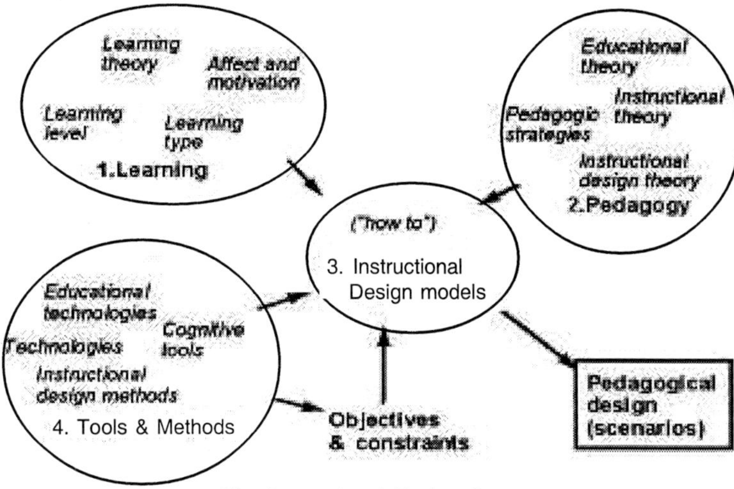

The Instructional Design Space

information processing or cognitive load, why metacognition and collaborative learning is important etc.

From a Fundamental Research Perspective

Many researchers in the field rather adopt a more fundamental research stance and they focus on small well defined problems such as "under which conditions can multimedia animations be effective."

From an Institutional Perspective

A field is implicitly defined by journals, conferences and study programmes.

The *Journal of Interactive Learning Research* published by the association for the Advancement of Computing in Education included the following enumeration of interactive learning environments that gives an idea on the technical scope of the field.

- authoring systems
- cognitive tools for learning

- computer-assisted language learning
- computer-based assessment systems
- computer-based training
- computer-mediated communications
- computer-supported collaborative learning
- distributed learning environments
- electronic performance support systems
- interactive learning environments
- interactive multimedia systems
- interactive simulations and games
- intelligent agents on the Internet
- intelligent tutoring systems
- microworlds
- virtual reality based learning systems

From a Technology Perspective

Each time a new technology appears soon after it may be hailed as a new solution to education by both researchers and practitioners. Therefore, one also could argue that fundamentally speaking, educational technology research and practice is technology driven (although not many members of the community would accept this stance).

From a "Where is it used Perspective"

- Distance education
- Blended learning
- Technology-enhanced classrooms (at all school levels)
- Informal learning (of various sorts)

Educational technology in way could be traced back to the emergence of very early tools, e.g., paintings on cave walls. But usually its history is made to start with educational film (1900's) or Sidney Pressey's mechanical teaching machines in the 1920'.

First large scale usage of new technologies can be traced to US WWII training of soldiers through training films and other mediated materials. Today, presentation-based technology, based on the idea that people can learn contents trough aural and visual reception, exists in many forms, e.g., streaming audio and video, PowerPoint presentations + voice-over.

The 1950's led to two major still popular designs. Skinners work led to "programmed instruction" focusing on the formulation of behavioral objectives, breaking instructional content into small units and rewarding correct responses early and often. Advocating a mastery approach to learning based on his taxonomy of intellectual behaviors, Bloom endorsed instructional techniques that varied both instruction and time according to learner requirements. Models based on these designs were usually referred to as computer-based training" (CBT), Computer-aided instruction or computer-assisted instruction (CAI) in the 1970's through the 1990's. In a more simplified form they correspond to today's "e-contents" that often form the core of "e-learning" set-ups, sometimes also referred to as web-based training (WBT) or e-instruction. The course designer divides learning contents into smaller chunks of text augmented with graphics and multimedia presentation. Frequent Multiple Choice questions with immediate feedback are added for self-assessment and guidance. Such e-contents can rely on standards defined by IMS, ADL/Scorm and IEEE.

The 1980's and 1990's produced a variety of schools that can be put under the umbrella of the label Computer-based learning (CBL). Frequently based on constructivist and cognitivist learning theories, these environments focused on teaching both abstract and domain-specific problem solving. Preferred technologies were micro-worlds (computer environments were learners could explore and build), simulations (computer environments where learner can play with parameters of dynamic systems) and hypertext.

Digitized communication and networking in education started in the mid 80s and became popular by the mid-90's, in particular through the World-Wide Web (WWW), eMail and Forums. There is a difference between two major forms of online learning. The earlier type, based on either Computer Based Training (CBT) or Computer-based learning (CBL), focused on the interaction between the student and computer drills plus tutorials on one hand or micro-worlds and simulations on the other. Both can be delivered today over the WWW. Today, the prevailing paradigm in the regular school system is Computer-mediated communication (CMC), where the primary form of interaction is between students and instructors, mediated by the computer. CBT/CBL usually means individualized (self-study) learning, while CMC involves teacher/tutor facilitation and requires scenarization of flexible learning activities. In addition, modern ICT provides education with tools for sustaining learning communities and associated knowledge management tasks. It also provides tools for student and curriculum management.

In addition to classroom enhancement, learning technologies also play a major role in full-time distance teaching. While most quality offers still rely on paper, videos and occasional CBT/CBL materials, there is increased use of e-tutoring through forums, instant messaging, video-conferencing etc. Courses addressed to smaller groups frequently use blended or hybrid designs that mix presence courses (usually in the beginning and at the end of a module) with distance activities and use various pedagogical styles (e.g., drill & practise, exercises, projects, etc.).

The 2000's emergence of multiple mobile and ubiquitous technologies gave a new impulse to situated learning theories favoring learning-in-context scenarios. Some literature uses the concept of integrated learning to describe blended learning scenarios that integrate both school and authentic (e.g., workplace) settings.

Families of Educational Technologies from a Conceptual Perspective

Today, we are facing a wide range of pedagogical strategies and available technologies. Classification schemes taking into account both dimensions can become very complex. We will present both simple and more complex attempts, but also take into account that pedagogical designs and technologies can be combined in certain ways, e.g., one can integrate activity-oriented courseware like a simulation within an content-oriented LMS.

Content *vs.* Communication

We distinguish between two big families: (1) content or courseware oriented and (2) communication/activity oriented. This typology reflects fundamentally different stances that can be found as well in research and practice.

1. Courseware oriented
   - (a) ***Contents with low interactivity:*** computer-based training (CBT), web-based training (WBT), Multimedia, main-stream E-learning including Learning technology systems like LMSs.
   - (b) ***Activity oriented:*** Computer-based learning, Microworlds, Simulations, Hypertext, (some) CSCL, Intelligent tutoring systems
2. Computer-mediated communication (CMC) oriented
   - (a) ***Activity-based and community oriented:*** C3MS (Community portals), Wikis where students write.

(b) ***Activity-based:*** LMSs like Moodle, Groupware,

(c) ***Cognitive tools:*** (some) CSCL, e.g., Writing-to-learn tools like Knowledge forum

(d) ***Communication tools*** (often combined with others): Instant messaging, Forums, Videoconferencing

This distinction is similar to Schulmeister's e-learning types A and B.

Design Methodologies and Research Approaches

Researchers in educational technology adopt different stances of what it means to practice academic research. One may initially distinguish a series of levels going from the conceptual to the technical:

1. Fundamental research: Many researchers in the field choose to adopt a more fundamental research stance focusing on small well-defined problems such as "under which conditions can multimedia animations be effective".

2. Technology-supported instructional design applied to various domains of education; major categories are distance teaching, blended teaching, computer-enhanced classroom teaching, industrial training.

   Other specializations may concern subject matters (e.g. science or language teaching) or approaches (direct instruction *vs.* project-oriented learning for example).

3. Research on the design and application of technologies. Researcher may specialize on subjects like the use of computer simulations in education or more technically, how to build authoring and learning environments for simulations.

Some researchers may combine a fundamental research perspective with a particular kind of instructional design and a particular kind of technology. Depending upon these options, research interests and research methodology will not be the same. From the possible combinations there are probably two major strands of thought that can be identified:

- Educational technology as part of the learning sciences. Research is inspired by and contributes to modern learning theory. This strand includes research communities like computer-supported collaborative learning, intelligent tutoring systems, ubiquitous computing.
- Educational technology as instructional technology. It is inspired by and contributes to instructional design theory and methodology. This strand includes research communities on e-learning, distance teaching, multimedia design.

Educational technology can be considered as a design science and as such, it has developed some specific research methodology like "Design-based research". However, since it addresses also all fundamental issues of learning, teaching and social organization, educational technology makes use of the full range of modern social science and life sciences methodology. Globally speaking, research methodology for educational technology relies on general research methodology, in particular on approaches of the social sciences.

EDUCATIONAL TECHNOLOGY AND THE HUMANITIES

Research from the Alberta Initiative for School Improvement (AISI) indicates that inquiry and project-based approaches, combined with a focus on curriculum, effectively supports the infusion of educational technologies into the learning and teaching process.

Technology in the Classroom

There are many kinds of computer and non-computer technologies currently in use in traditional classrooms. Among these are:

- **Computer in the Classroom:** Having a computer in the classroom is an asset to any teacher. With a computer in the classroom, teachers are able to demonstrate a new lesson, present new material, illustrate how to use new programmes, and show new websites.

- **Class Website:** What better way to display your student's work, than to create a web page designed just for your class. Once a web page is designed, teachers can post homework assignments, student work, famous quotes, trivia games, and so much more. In current day society, children know how to use the computer and navigate their way through a website, so why not give them one where they can be a published author. Just be careful as most districts maintain strong policies to manage official websites for a school or classroom.

- **Class Blogs and Wikis:** These are some of a variety of Web 2.0 tools that are currently being implemented in the classroom. Blogs allow for students to maintain a running dialogue, like a journal, of thoughts, ideas, and assignments that also provide for student comment and reiterative reflection. Wikis are more group focused to allow multiple members of the group to edit a single document and create a truly collaborative and carefully edited finished product.

- **Wireless Classroom Microphones:** Noisy classrooms are a daily occurrence, and with the help of microphones, students are able to hear their teachers clearer. Children learn better when they hear the teacher clearly. The benefit for teachers is that they no longer lose their voices at the end of the day.

- **Mobile devices:** Mobile devices such as clickers or smartphone can be used to enhance the experience in the classroom by providing the possibility for professors to get feedback. (read more in the article MLearning).

There are many other tools being utilized depending on the local school board and fund availability. These may include: digital cameras, video cameras, interactive whiteboard tools, document cameras, or LCD projectors.

Societies

Learned societies concerned with educational technology include:

- Association for the Advancement of Computing in Education (AACE)
- Association for Educational Communications and Technology
- Association for Learning Technology
- International Society for Technology in Education - (ISTE)
- Northwest Council for Computer Education
- Computer-Using Educators

2

Instructional Design and Technology

Instructional Design (also called Instructional Systems Design (ISD)) is the practice of maximizing the effectiveness, efficiency and appeal of instruction and other learning experiences. The process consists broadly of determining the current state and needs of the learner, defining the end goal of instruction, and creating some "intervention" to assist in the transition. Ideally the process is informed by pedagogically and andragogically (adult learning) tested theories of learning and may take place in student-only, teacher-led or community-based settings. The outcome of this instruction may be directly observable and scientifically measured or completely hidden and assumed. There are many instructional design models but many are based on the ADDIE model with the phases analyzis, design, development, implementation, and evaluation. As a field, instructional design is historically and traditionally rooted in cognitive and behavioral psychology.

Much of the foundation of the field of instructional design was laid in World War II, when the U.S. military faced the need to rapidly train large numbers of people to perform complex technical tasks, from field-stripping a carbine to navigating across the ocean to building a bomber—see "Training Within Industry (TWI)". Drawing on the research and theories of B.F. Skinner on operant conditioning, training programmes focused on observable behaviors. Tasks were broken down into subtasks, and each subtask treated as a separate learning goal. Training was designed to reward correct performance and remediate incorrect performance. Mastery was assumed to be possible for every learner, given enough repetition and feedback. After the war, the success of the wartime training model was replicated in business and industrial training, and to a lesser extent in the primary and secondary classroom. The approach is still common in the U.S. military.

In 1956, a committee lead by Benjamin Bloom published an influential taxonomy of what he termed the three domains of learning: Cognitive (what one knows or thinks), Psychomotor (what one does, physically) and Affective (what one feels, or what attitudes one has). These taxonomies still influence the design of instruction.

During the latter half of the 20th century, learning theories began to be influenced by the growth of digital computers.

In the 1970s, many instructional design theorists began to adopt an information-processing-based approach to the design of instruction. David Merrill for instance developed Component Display Theory (CDT), which concentrates on the means of presenting instructional materials (presentation techniques).

Later in the 1980s and throughout the 1990s cognitive load theory began to find empirical support for a variety of presentation techniques.

Cognitive Load Theory and the Design of Instruction

Cognitive load theory developed out of several empirical studies of learners, as they interacted with instructional materials. Sweller and his associates began to measure the effects of working memory load, and found that the format of instructional materials has a direct effect on the performance of the learners using those materials.

While the media debates of the 1990s focused on the influences of media on learning, cognitive load effects were being documented in several journals. Rather than attempting to substantiate the use of media, these cognitive load learning effects provided an empirical basis for the use of instructional strategies. Mayer asked the instructional design community to reassess the media debate, to refocus their attention on what was most important–learning.

By the mid to late 1990s, Sweller and his associates had discovered several learning effects related to cognitive load and the design of instruction (e.g. the split attention effect, redundancy effect, and the worked-example effect). Later, other researchers like Richard Mayer began to attribute learning effects to cognitive load. Mayer and his associates soon developed a Cognitive Theory of Multimedia Learning.

In the past decade, cognitive load theory has begun to be internationally accepted and begun to revolutionize how practitioners of instructional design view instruction. Recently, human performance experts have even taken notice of cognitive load theory, and have begun to promote this theory base as the science of instruction, with instructional designers as the practitioners of this field. Finally Clark, Nguyen and Sweller published a textbook describing how Instructional Designers can promote efficient learning using evidence based guidelines of Cognitive load theory?

Instructional Designers use various instructional strategies to reduce cognitive load. For example, they think that the onscreen text should not be more than 150 words or the text should be presented in small meaningful chunks. The designers also use auditory and visual methods to communicate information to the learner.

Learning Design

The IMS Learning Design specification supports the use of a wide range of pedagogies in online learning. Rather than attempting to capture the specifics of many pedagogies, it does this by providing a generic and flexible language. This language is designed to enable many different pedagogies to be expressed. The approach has the advantage over alternatives in that only one set of learning design and runtime tools then need to be implemented in order to support the desired wide range of pedagogies. The language was originally developed at the Open University of the Netherlands, after extensive examination and comparison of a wide range of pedagogical approaches and their associated learning activities, and several iterations of the developing language to obtain a good balance between generality and pedagogic expressiveness.

A criticism of Learning Design theory is that learning is an outcome. While instructional theory Instructional Design focuses on outcomes, while properly accounting for a multi-variate context that can only be predictive, it acknowledges that (given the variabilities in human capability) a guarantee of reliable learning outcomes is improbable. We can only design instruction. We cannot design learning (an outcome). Automotive engineers can design a car that, under specific conditions, will achieve 50 miles per gallon. These engineers cannot guarantee that drivers of the cars they design will (or have the capability to) operate these vehicles according to the specific conditions prescribed. The former is the metaphor for instructional design. The latter is the metaphor for Learning Design.

Instructional Design Models

ADDIE Model

Perhaps the most common model used for creating instructional materials is the ADDIE Model. This acronym stands for the 5 phases contained in the model:

- **Analyze** - analyze learner characteristics, task to be learned, etc.

- **Design** - develop learning objectives, choose an instructional approach
- **Develop** - create instructional or training materials
- **Implement** - deliver or distribute the instructional materials
- **Evaluate** - make sure the materials achieved the desired goals

Most of the current instructional design models are variations of the ADDIE model.

Rapid Prototyping

A sometimes utilized adaptation to the ADDIE model is in a practice known as rapid prototyping.

However, rapid prototyping is considered a somewhat simplistic type of model. At the heart of Instructional Design is the analysis phase. After you thoroughly conduct the analysis—you can then choose a model based on your findings. That is the area where most people get snagged—they simply do not do a thorough enough analysis.

Proponents suggest that through an iterative process the verification of the design documents saves time and money by catching problems while they are still easy to fix. This approach is not novel to the design of instruction, but appears in many design-related domains including software design, architecture, transportation planning, product development, message design, user experience design, etc.

Dick and Carey

Another well-known instructional design model is **The Dick and Carey Systems Approach Model**. The model was originally published in 1978 by Walter Dick and Lou Carey in their book entitled The Systematic Design of Instruction.

Dick and Carey made a significant contribution to the instructional design field by championing a systems view of instruction as opposed to viewing instruction as a sum of isolated parts. The model addresses instruction as an entire system, focusing on the interrelationship between context, content, learning and instruction. According to Dick and Carey, "Components such as the instructor, learners, materials, instructional activities, delivery system, and learning and performance environments interact with each other and work together to bring about the desired student learning outcomes". The components of the Systems Approach Model, also known as the Dick and Carey Model, are as follows:

- Identify Instructional Goal(s)
- Conduct Instructional Analyzis
- Analyze Learners and Contexts
- Write Performance Objectives
- Develop Assessment Instruments
- Develop Instructional Strategy
- Develop and Select Instructional Materials
- Design and Conduct Formative Evaluation of Instruction
- Revise Instruction
- Design and Conduct Summative Evaluation

With this model, components are executed iteratively and in parallel rather than linearly.

Instructional Development Learning System (IDLS)

Another instructional design model is the **Instructional Development Learning System (IDLS)**. The model was originally published in 1970 by Peter J. Esseff, Ph.D. and Mary Sullivan Esseff, Ph.D. in their book entitled *IDLS—Pro Trainer 1: How to Design, Develop, and Validate Instructional Materials*].

Peter & Mary Esseff both received their doctorates in Educational Technology from the Catholic University of America under the mentorship of Dr. Gabriel Ofiesh, a Founding Father of the Military Model mentioned above. Esseff and Esseff contributed synthesized existing theories to develop their approach to systematic design, "Instructional Development Learning System" (IDLS).

The components of the IDLS Model are:

- Design a Task Analyzis
- Develop Criterion Tests and Performance Measures
- Develop Interactive Instructional Materials
- Validate the Interactive Instructional Materials

Other Models

Some other useful models of instructional design include: the Smith/Ragan Model, the Morrison/Ross/Kemp Model and the OAR model.

Learning theories also play an important role in the design of instructional materials. Theories such as behaviourism, constructivism, social learning and cognitivism help shape and define the outcome of instructional materials.

INSTRUCTIONAL SCAFFOLDING

Instructional scaffolding is the provision of sufficient support to promote learning when concepts and skills are being first introduced to students. These supports may include the following:

- Resources
- A compelling task
- Templates and guides
- Guidance on the development of cognitive and social skills

These supports are gradually removed as students develop autonomous learning strategies, thus promoting their own cognitive, affective and psychomotor learning skills and knowledge. Teachers help the students master a task or a concept by providing support. The support can take many forms such as outlines, recommended documents, storyboards, or key questions.

Scaffolding Theory was first introduced in the late 1950s by Jerome Bruner, a cognitive psychologist. He used the term to describe young children's oral language acquisition. Helped by their parents when they first start learning to speak, young children are provided with instinctive structures to learn a language. Bed-time stories and read alouds are classic examples. Wood, Bruner, and Ross' (1976) idea of scaffolding also parallels Vygotsky's work. Though the term was never used by Vygotsky, interactional support and the process by which adults mediate a child's attempts to take on new learning has come to be termed "scaffolding." Scaffolding represents the helpful interactions between adult and child that enable the child to do something beyond his or her independent efforts. A scaffold is a temporary framework that is put up for support and access to meaning and taken away as needed when the child secures control of success with a task. Cazden defined a scaffold as "a temporary framework for construction in progress". For example, parents seem to know intuitively how to scaffold their children's attempts at negotiating meaning through oral language. The construction of a scaffold occurs at a time where the child may not be able to articulate or explore learning independently. The scaffolds provided by the tutor do not change the nature or difficulty level of the task; instead, the scaffolds provided allow the student to successfully complete the task.

In writing instruction, typically support is presented in verbal form (discourse). The writing tutor engages the learner's attention, calibrates the task, motivates the student, identifies relevant task feature, controls for frustration, and demonstrates as needed. Through joint activities, the teacher scaffolds conversation to maximize the development of a child's intrapsychological functioning. In this process, the adult controls the elements of the task that are beyond the child's ability all the while increasing the expectations of what the child is able to do. Speech, a critical tool to scaffold thinking and responding, plays a crucial role in the development of higher psychological processes because it enables thinking to be more abstract, flexible, and independent. From a Vygotskian perspective, talk and action work together with the sociocultural fabric of the writing event to shape a child's construction of awareness and performance. Dialogue may range from casual talk to deliberate explanations about features of written language. The talk embedded in the actions of the literacy event shapes the child's learning as the tutor regulates her language to conform to the child's degrees of understanding. Clay shows that what may seem like casual conversational exchanges between tutor and student actually offer many opportunities for fostering cognitive development, language learning, story composition for writing, and reading comprehension. Conversations facilitate generative, constructive, experimental, and developmental speech and writing in the development of new ideas.

Children use oral language as a vehicle for discovering and negotiating emergent written language and understandings for getting meaning on paper. Writing and speech as tools can lead to discovery of new thinking. The teacher offers levels of verbal and non-verbal demonstrations and directions as the child observes, mimics, or shares the writing task. With increased understanding and control, the child needs less assistance. The teacher's level and type of support change over time from directive, to suggestion, to encouragement, to observation. Optimum scaffolds adapt to the child's tempo moving from other-regulation to self-regulation. The child eventually provides self-scaffolding through internal thought. Within these scaffolding events, teaching and learning, inseparable components, emphasize both the child's personal construction of literacy and the adult's contributions to the child's developing understandings of print. The child contributes what she can and the adult contributes so as to sustain the task.

Using a Vygotskian theoretical framework, Wertsch and Stone examine scaffolded instruction in a one-to-one remedial clinic setting with a learning disabled child. The researchers show how adult language directs the child to strategically monitor actions. Analysis of communicative patterns show a transition and progression in the source of strategic responsibility from teacher or other-regulated to child or self-regulated behaviours. In Vygotsky's words, "what the child is able to do in collaboration today he will be able to do independently tomorrow".

Some ingredients of scaffolding are predictability, playfulness, focus on meaning, role reversal, modeling, and nomenclature.

Levels and Types of Scaffolding in the Educational Setting

According to Saye and Brush, there are two levels of scaffolding: soft and hard. An example of soft scaffolding in the classroom would be when a teacher circulates the room and converses with his or her students. The teacher may question their approach to a difficult problem and provide constructive feedback. According to Van Lier, this type of scaffolding can also be referred to as contingent scaffolding. The type and amount of support needed is dependent on the needs of the students during the time of instruction. Unfortunately, scaffolding can be difficult when the classroom is large and students have various needs.

On the other hand, hard scaffolds are developed in order to assist students with a difficult task. The key is that the assistance is planned in advance. For example, when students are discovering the formula for the Pythagorean Theorem in math class, the teacher may identify hints or cues to help the student reach an even higher level of thinking. In both situations, the idea of "expert scaffolding" is being implemented. In the example given above, the teacher in the classroom is considered as the expert and responsible for the scaffolding of his or her students.

Reciprocal scaffolding, a method first coined by Holton and Thomas, is a method that involves a group of two or more collaboratively working together. In this situation, the group can learn from each other's experiences and knowledge. The scaffolding is shared by each member and changes constantly as the group work on a task. According to Vygotsky, students develop higher-level thinking skills when scaffolding occurs with an adult expert or with a peer of higher capabilities. Conversely, Piaget believes that students discard their ideas when paired with an adult or student of more expertise. Instead, students should be paired with others who have different perspectives. Conflicts would then take place between students allowing them to think constructively at a higher level.

Technical scaffolding is a newer approach in which computers replace the teachers as the experts or guides, and students can be guided with web links, online tutorials, or help pages. Educational software can help students follow a clear structure and allows students to plan properly.

Scaffolding and Problem-based Learning in the Educational Setting

Scaffolding is often used in order to support problem-based learning (PBL). Learners in the classroom become researchers and often work in small groups to analyze problems, determine solutions, and evaluate problems when utilizing PBL. In one study, PBL with medical students was proven to develop a deeper understanding, improve retention of material, and increase overall attitude when compared to other students who did not receive PBL. Many educators incorporate PBL in their classrooms in order to engage students and help them become better problem solvers. Scaffolding may help the success of PBL in the classroom. Teachers must identify the content that needs scaffolding (support), the appropriate time to implement the support, a method to follow, and determine when the scaffold can be removed.

INSTRUCTIONAL TECHNOLOGY

In education, **instructional technology** is "the theory and practice of design, development, utilization, management, and evaluation of processes and resources for learning," according to the Association for Educational Communications and Technology (AECT) Definitions and Terminology Committee. Instructional technology is often referred to as a part of educational technology. While instructional technology covers the processes and systems of learning and instruction, educational technology includes other systems used in the process of developing human capability.

The first use of instructional technology cannot be attributed to a specific person or time. Many histories of instructional technology start in the early 1900s, while others go back to the 1600s. This depends on the definition of *instructional technology*. Definitions that focus on a systems approach tend to reach further back in history, while those definitions focused on sensory devices are more recent.

The use of audio and visual instruction was boosted as a military response to the problems of a labour shortage during WWII in the United States. There was a definitive need to fill the factories with skilled labour. Instructional technology provided a methodology for training in a systematic and efficient manner.

With it came the use of highly structured manuals, instructional films, and standardized tests. Thomas Edison saw the value of instructional technology in films but did not formalize the science of instruction as the US military did so well.

Current Status

Instructional technology is a growing field of study which uses technology as a means to solve educational challenges, both in the classroom and in distance learning environments.

While instructional technology promises solutions to many educational problems, resistance from faculty and administrators to the use of technology in the classroom is not unusual. This reaction can arise from the belief — or fear — that the ultimate aim of instructional technology is to reduce or even remove the human element of instruction. However, most instructional technologists would counter that education will always require human intervention from instructors or facilitators.

Many graduate programmes are producing instructional designers, who increasingly are being employed by industry and universities to create materials for distance education programmes. These professionals often employ e-learning tools, which provide distance learners the opportunity to interact with instructors and experts in the field, even if they are not located physically close to each other.

More recently a new form of Instructional technology known as Human Performance Technology has evolved. HPT focuses on performance problems and deals primarily with corporate entities.

Relation to Learning Theory

The purpose of instructional technology, of course, is the promotion of learning. Learning theory (education) has influenced Instructional design and Instructional designers (the practitioners of Instructional Technology). Instructional Technologies promote communication and interactivity. These two come together under the general heading of Interaction.

Moore argues that there are three types of learner interaction (learner-content, learner-instructor, and learner-learner interactions). In the years since Moore's article, several philosophical views have surfaced that relate Instructional technology to these types of interaction.

Most traditional researchers (those subscribing to Cognitivism) argue that learner-content interaction is perhaps the most important endeavour of Instructional technology. Some researchers (those subscribing to constructivism) argue that Moore's social interactions, (learner-instructor and learner-learner interactions), are as useful as learner-content interaction.

Areas

Razavi advocates that educational technology covers instructional technology. It includes instructional technology and the field study in human teaching and learning. So educational technology is broader than instructional technology. Instructional technology itself is consisted from two major parts. One is teaching technology and another is learning technology. In the education industry, the term "instructional technology" is frequently used interchangeably with "educational technology."

Human Performance Technology (HPT) has a focus on corporate environments. Learning sciences are a growing area of focus dealing instructional techniques and learning theories.

●●

3
E-Learning

E-learning (or electronic learning or eLearning) is a term that encompasses all forms of Technology-Enhanced Learning (TEL) or very specific types of TEL such as online or Web-based learning. Nevertheless, the term does not have a universally accepted definition and there are divides in the e-learning industry about whether a technology-enhanced system can be called e-learning if there is no set pedagogy as some argue e-learning is: "pedagogy empowered by digital technology".

The term e-learning is ambiguous to those outside the e-learning industry, and even within its diverse disciplines it has different meanings to different people. For instance, in companies, it often refers to the strategies that use the company network to deliver training courses to employees and lately in most Universities, e-learning is used to define a specific mode to attend a course or program of study where the students rarely or never meet face-to-face, nor access on-campus educational facilities, because they study online.

Goals and Benefits of E-Learning

E-Learning can provide benefits for the organizations and individuals involved.

1. **Improved performance**: A 12-year meta-analysis of research by the U.S. Department of Education found that higher education students in online learning generally performed better than those in face-to-face courses.

2. **Increased access:** Instructors of the highest calibre can share their knowledge across borders, allowing students to attend courses across physical, political, and economic boundaries. Recognized experts have the opportunity of making information available internationally, to anyone interested at minimum costs. For example, the MIT OpenCourseWare program has made substantial portions of that university's curriculum and lectures available for free online.
3. **Convenience and flexibility to learners:** in many contexts, e-learning is self-paced and the learning sessions are available 24x7. Learners are not bound to a specific day/time to physically attend classes. They can also pause learning sessions at their convenience.The High technology is not necessary for all online courses. Basic internet access, audio, and video capabilities are common requirements.
4. **To develop the skills and competencies needed in the 21st century, in particular to ensure that learners have the digital literacy skills required in their discipline, profession or career** Bates (2009) states that a major argument for e-learning is that it enables learners to develop essential skills for knowledge-based workers by embedding the use of information and communications technologies within the curriculum. He also argues that using e-learning in this way has major implications for course design and the assessment of learners.

Market

The worldwide e-learning industry is estimated to be worth over thirty-eight (38) billion euros according to conservative estimates, although in the European Union only about 20% of e-learning products are produced within the common market . Developments in internet and multimedia technologies are the basic enabler of e-learning, with consulting, content, technologies, services and support being identified as the five key sectors of the e-learning industry.

Higher Education

By 2006, nearly 3.5 million students were participating in on-line learning at institutions of higher education in the United States. According to the Sloan Foundation reports, there has been an increase of around 12-14 per cent per year on average in enrollments for fully online learning over the five years 2004-2009 in the US post-secondary system, compared with an average of approximately 2 per cent increase per year in enrollments overall. Allen and Seamen (2009) claim that almost a quarter of all students in post-secondary education were taking fully online courses in 2008, and a report by Ambient Insight Research suggests that in 2009, 44 per cent of post-secondary students in the USA were taking some or all of their courses online, and projected that this figure would rise to 81 per cent by 2014. Thus it can be seen that e-learning is moving rapidly from the margins to being a predominant form of post-secondary education, at least in the USA.

Many higher education, for-profit institutions, now offer on-line classes. By contrast, only about half of private, non-profit schools offer them. The Sloan report, based on a poll of academic leaders, says that students generally appear to be at least as satisfied with their on-line classes as they are with traditional ones. Private institutions may become more involved with on-line presentations as the cost of instituting such a system decreases. Properly trained staff must also be hired to work with students on-line. These staff members need to understand the content area, and also be highly trained in the use of the computer and Internet. Online education is rapidly increasing, and online doctoral programmes have even developed at leading research universities.

Early E-Learning systems, based on Computer-Based Learning/Training often attempted to replicate autocratic teaching styles whereby the role of the e-learning system was assumed to be for transferring knowledge, as opposed to systems developed later based on Computer Supported Collaborative Learning (CSCL), which encouraged the shared development of knowledge.

As early as 1993, **Graziadei**, W. D. described an online computer-delivered lecture, tutorial and assessment project using electronic Mail, two VAX Notes conferences and Gopher/ Lynx together with several software programs that allowed students and instructor to create a Virtual Instructional Classroom Environment in Science (VICES) in Research, Education, Service & Teaching (REST). In 1997 Graziadei, W.D., et al., published an article entitled "Building Asynchronous and Synchronous Teaching-Learning Environments: Exploring a Course/Classroom Management System Solution". They described a process at the State University of New York (SUNY) of evaluating products and developing an overall strategy for technology-based course development and management in teaching-learning. The product(s) had to be easy to use and maintain, portable, replicable, scalable, and immediately affordable, and they had to have a high probability of success with long-term cost-effectiveness. Today many technologies can be, and are, used in e-Learning, from blogs to collaborative software, ePortfolios, and virtual classrooms. Most eLearning situations use combinations of these techniques.

E-Learning 2.0

The term E-Learning 2.0 is a neologism for CSCL systems that came about during the emergence of Web 2.0. From an E-Learning 2.0 perspective, conventional e-learning systems were based on instructional packets, which were delivered to students using Internet technologies. The role of the student consisted in learning from the readings and preparing assignments. Assignments were evaluated by the teacher. In contrast, the new e-learning places increased emphasis on social learning and use of social software such as blogs, wikis, podcasts and virtual worlds such as Second Life. This phenomenon has also been referred to as Long Tail Learning.

E-Learning 2.0, by contrast to e-learning systems not based on CSCL, assumes that knowledge (as meaning and understanding) is socially constructed. Learning takes place through conversations about content and grounded interaction about problems and actions. Advocates of social learning claim that one of the best ways to learn something is to teach it to others.

However, it should be noted that many early online courses, such as those developed by Murray Turoff and Roxanne Hiltz in the 1970s and 80s at the New Jersey Institute of Technology, courses at the University of Guelph in Canada, the British Open University, and the online distance courses at the University of British Columbia (where Web CT, now incorporated into Blackboard Inc. was first developed), have always made heavy use of online discussion between students. Also, from the start, practitioners such as Harasim (1995) have put heavy emphasis on the use of learning networks for knowledge construction, long before the term e-learning, let alone e-learning 2.0, was even considered.

There is also an increased use of virtual classrooms (online presentations delivered live) as an online learning platform and classroom for a diverse set of education providers such as Minnesota State Colleges and Universities and Sachem School District.

In addition to virtual classroom environments, social networks have become an important part of E-learning 2.0. Social networks have been used to foster online learning communities around subjects as diverse as test preparation and language education. Mobile Assisted Language Learning (MALL) is a term used to describe using handheld computers or cell phones to assist in language learning.

Approaches to E-Learning Services

E-learning services have evolved since computers were first used in education. There is a trend to move toward blended learning services, where computer-based activities are integrated with practical or classroom-based situations.

Bates and Poole (2003) and the OECD (2005) suggest that different types or forms of e-learning can be considered as a continuum, from no e-learning, i.e. no use of computers and/or the Internet for teaching and learning, through classroom aids, such as making classroom lecture Powerpoint slides available to students through a course web site or learning management system, to laptop programs, where students are required to bring laptops to class and use them as part of a face-to-face class, to hybrid learning, where classroom time is reduced but not eliminated, with more time devoted to online learning, through to fully online learning, which is a form of distance education. This classification is somewhat similar to that of the Sloan Commission reports on the status of e-learning, which refer to web enhanced, web supplemented and web dependent to reflect increasing intensity of technology use.In the Bates and Poole continuum, 'blended learning' can cover classroom aids, laptops and hybrid learning, while 'distributed learning' can incorporate either hybrid or fully online learning.

It can be seen then that e-learning can describe a wide range of applications, and it is often by no means clear even in peer reviewed research publications which form of e-learning is being discussed. However, Bates and Poole argue that when instructors say they are using e-learning, this most often refers to the use of technology as classroom aids, although over time, there has been a gradual increase in fully online learning.

Computer-Based Learning

Computer-based learning, sometimes abbreviated to CBL, refers to the use of computers as a key component of the educational environment. While this can refer to the use of computers in a classroom, the term more broadly refers to a structured environment in which computers are used for teaching purposes. The concept is generally seen as being distinct from the use of computers in ways where learning is at least a peripheral element of the experience (e.g. computer games and web browsing).

Computer-Based Training

Computer-Based Trainings (CBTs) are self-paced learning activities accessible via a computer or handheld device. CBTs typically present content in a linear fashion, much like reading an online book or manual. For this reason they are often used to teach static processes, such as using software or completing mathematical equations. The term Computer-Based Training is often used interchangeably with Web-based training (WBT) with the primary difference being the delivery method. Where CBTs are typically delivered via CD-ROM, WBTs are delivered via the Internet using a web browser. Assessing learning in a CBT usually comes in the form of multiple choice questions, or other assessments that can be easily scored by a computer.

CBTs can be a good alternative to printed learning materials since rich media, including videos or animations, can easily be embedded to enhance the learning. Another advantage to CBTs are that they can be easily distributed to a wide audience at a relatively low cost once the initial development is completed.

However, CBTs pose some learning challenges as well. Typically the creation of effective CBTs requires enormous resources. The software for developing CBTs (such as Flash or Adobe Director) is often more complex than a subject matter expert or teacher is able to use. In addition, the lack of human interaction can limit both the type of content that can be presented as well as the type of assessment that can be performed. Many learning organizations are beginning to use smaller CBT/WBT activities as part of a broader online learning program which may include online discussion or other interactive elements.

Computer-Supported Collaborative Learning (CSCL)

Computer-supported collaborative learning (CSCL) is one of the most promising innovations to improve teaching and learning with the help of modern information and communication technology. Most recent developments in CSCL have been called E-Learning 2.0, but the concept of collaborative or group learning whereby instructional methods are designed to encourage or require students to work together on learning tasks has existed much longer. It is widely agreed to distinguish collaborative learning from the traditional 'direct transfer' model in which the instructor is assumed to be the distributor of knowledge and skills, which is often given the neologism, E-Learning 1.0, even though this direct transfer method most accurately reflects Computer-Based Learning systems (CBL).

In Datacloud: Toward a New Theory of Online Work, Johndan Johnson-Eilola describes a specific computer-supported collaboriatin space: The Smart Board. According to Johnson-Eilola, a "Smart Board system provides a 72-inch, rear projection, touchscreen, intelligent whiteboard surface for work". In Datacloud, Johnson-Eilola asserts that "e are attempting to understand how users move within information spaces, how users can exist within information spaces rather than merely gaze at them, and how information spaces must be shared with others rather than being private, lived within rather than simply visited". He explains how the Smart Board system offers an information space that allows his students to engage in active collaboration. He makes three distinct claims regarding the functionality of the technology: (1) The Smart Board allows users to work with large amounts of information, (2) It offers an information space that invites active collaboration, 3) The work produced is often "dynamic and contingent".

Johnson-Eilola further explains that with the Smart Board "...information work becom a bodied experience". Users have the opportunity to engage with—inhabit—the technology by direct manipulation. Moreover, this space allows for more than one user; essentially, it invites multiple users.

Technology-Enhanced Learning (TEL)

Technology enhanced learning (TEL) has the goal to provide socio-technical innovations (also improving efficiency and cost effectiveness) for e-learning practices, regarding individuals and organizations, independent of time, place and pace. The field of TEL therefore applies to the support of any learning activity through technology.

Technology Issues

Along with the terms learning technology, instructional technology, and Educational Technology, the term is generally used to refer to the use of technology in learning in a much broader sense than the computer-based training or Computer Aided Instruction of the 1980s. It is also broader than the terms Online Learning or Online Education which generally refer to purely web-based learning. In cases where mobile technologies are used, the term M-learning has become more common. E-learning, however, also has implications beyond just the technology and refers to the actual learning that takes place using these systems.

E-learning is naturally suited to distance learning and flexible learning, but can also be used in conjunction with face-to-face teaching, in which case the term Blended learning is commonly used. E-Learning pioneer Bernard Luskin argues that the "E" must be understood to have broad meaning if e-Learning is to be effective. Luskin says that the "e" should be interpreted to mean exciting, energetic, enthusiastic, emotional, extended, excellent, and educational in addition to "electronic" that is a traditional national interpretation. This broader interpretation allows for 21st century applications and brings learning and media psychology into the equation.

In higher education especially, the increasing tendency is to create a Virtual Learning Environment (VLE) (which is sometimes combined with a Management Information System (MIS) to create a Managed Learning Environment) in which all aspects of a course are handled through a consistent user interface standard throughout the institution. A growing number of physical universities, as well as newer online-only colleges, have begun to offer a select set of academic degree and certificate programmes via the Internet at a wide range of levels and in a wide range of disciplines. While some programmes require students to attend some campus classes or orientations, many are delivered completely online. In addition, several universities offer online student support services, such as online advising and registration, e-counseling, online textbook purchase, student governments and student newspapers.

E-Learning can also refer to educational web sites such as those offering learning scenarios, worksheets and interactive exercises for children. The term is also used extensively in the business sector where it generally refers to cost-effective online training.

The recent trend in the e-Learning sector is screencasting. There are many screencasting tools available but the latest buzz is all about the web based screencasting tools which allow the users to create screencasts directly from their browser and make the video available online so that the viewers can stream the video directly. The advantage of such tools is that it gives the presenter the ability to show his ideas and flow of thoughts rather than simply explain them, which may be more confusing when delivered via simple text instructions. With the combination of video and audio, the expert can mimic the one on one experience of the classroom and deliver clear, complete instructions. From the learners point of view this provides the ability to pause and rewind and gives the learner the advantage to move at their own pace, something a classroom cannot always offer. One such example of e-Learning platform based on screencasts is YoHelpOnline.

Communication Technologies used in E-Learning

Communication technologies are generally categorized as asynchronous or synchronous. Asynchronous activities use technologies such as blogs, wikis, and discussion boards. The idea here is that participants may engage in the exchange of ideas or information without the dependency of other participants involvement at the same time. Electronic mail (Email) is also asynchronous in that mail can be sent or received without having both the participants' involvement at the same time.

Synchronous activities involve the exchange of ideas and information with one or more participants during the same period of time. A face to face discussion is an example of synchronous communications. Synchronous activities occur with all participants joining in at once, as with an online chat session or a virtual classroom or meeting.

Virtual classrooms and meetings can often use a mix of communication technologies.

In many models, the writing community and the communication channels relate with the E-learning and the

M-learning communities. Both the communities provide a general overview of the basic learning models and the activities required for the participants to join the learning sessions across the virtual classroom or even across standard classrooms enabled by technology. Many activities, essential for the learners in these environments, require frequent chat sessions in the form of virtual classrooms and/or blog meetings. Lately context-aware ubiquitous technology has been providing an innovative way for written and oral communications by using a mobile device with sensors and RFID readers and tags.

Learning Management System (LMS) and Learning Content Management System (LCMS)

A **learning management system** (LMS) is software for delivering, tracking and managing training/education. LMSs range from systems for managing training/educational records to software for distributing courses over the Internet and offering features for online collaboration.

A **learning content management system** (LCMS) is software for authoring, editing and indexing e-learning content (courses, reusable content objects). An LCMS may be solely dedicated to producing and publishing content that is hosted on an LMS, or it can host the content itself (remote AICC content hosting model).

Computer-Aided Assessment

Computer-aided Assessment (also but less commonly referred to as E-assessment), ranging from automated multiple-choice tests to more sophisticated systems is becoming increasingly common. With some systems, feedback can be geared towards a student's specific mistakes or the computer can navigate the student through a series of questions adapting to what the student appears to have learned or not learned.

The best examples follow a Formative Assessment structure and are called "Online Formative Assessment". This involves making an initial formative assessment by sifting out the incorrect answers. The author/teacher will then explain what the pupil should have done with each question. It will then give the pupil at least one practice at each slight variation of sifted out questions. This is the formative learning stage. The next stage is to make a Summative Assessment by a new set of questions only covering the topics previously taught. Some will take this even further and repeat the cycle such as BOFA which is aimed at the Eleven plus exam set in the UK.

The term learning design has sometimes come to refer to the type of activity enabled by software such as the open-source system LAMS which supports sequences of activities that can be both adaptive and collaborative. The IMS Learning Design specification is intended as a standard format for learning designs, and IMS LD Level A is supported in LAMS V2.elearning has been replacing the traditional settings due to its cost effectiveness.

Electronic Performance Support Systems (EPSS)

An Electronic performance support systems (EPSS) is a "computer-based system that improves worker productivity by providing on-the-job access to integrated information, advice, and learning experiences" Barry Raybould.

Content Issues

Content is a core component of e-learning and includes issues such as pedagogy and learning object re-use.

Pedagogical Elements

Pedagogical elements are an attempt to define structures or units of educational material. For example, this could be a lesson, an assignment, a multiple choice question, a quiz, a discussion group or a case study. These units should be format independent, so although it may be in any of the following methods, pedagogical structures would **not** include a textbook, a web page, a video conference or Podcast.

When beginning to create e-Learning content, the pedagogical approaches need to be evaluated. Simple pedagogical approaches make it easy to create content, but lack flexibility, richness and downstream functionality. On the other hand, complex pedagogical approaches can be difficult to set up and slow to develop, though they have the potential to provide more engaging learning experiences for students. Somewhere between these extremes is an ideal pedagogy that allows a particular educator to effectively create educational materials while simultaneously providing the most engaging educational experiences for students.

Pedagogical Approaches or Perspectives

It is possible to use various pedagogical approaches for eLearning which include:

- **Instructional design** - The traditional pedagogy of instruction which is curriculum focused, and is developed by a centralized educating group or a single teacher.
- **Social-constructivist** - This pedagogy is particularly well afforded by the use of discussion forums, blogs, wiki and on-line collaborative activities. It is a collaborative approach that opens educational content creation to a wider group including the students themselves. The One Laptop Per Child Foundation attempted to use a constructivist approach in its project.
- **Laurillard's Conversational Model** is also particularly relevant to eLearning, and Gilly Salmon's Five-Stage Model is a pedagogical approach to the use of discussion boards.

- **Cognitive perspective** focuses on the cognitive processes involved in learning as well as how the brain works.
- **Emotional perspective** focuses on the emotional aspects of learning, like motivation, engagement, fun, etc.
- **Behavioural perspective** focuses on the skills and behavioural outcomes of the learning process. Role-playing and application to on-the-job settings.
- **Contextual perspective** focuses on the environmental and social aspects which can stimulate learning. Interaction with other people, collaborative discovery and the importance of peer support as well as pressure.

Reusability, Standards and Learning Objects

Much effort has been put into the technical reuse of electronically-based teaching materials and in particular creating or re-using Learning Objects. These are self contained units that are properly tagged with keywords, or other metadata, and often stored in an XML file format. Creating a course requires putting together a sequence of learning objects. There are both proprietary and open, non-commercial and commercial, peer-reviewed repositories of learning objects such as the Merlot repository.

A common standard format for e-learning content is SCORM whilst other specifications allow for the transporting of "learning objects" (Schools Framework) or categorizing metadata (LOM).

These standards themselves are early in the maturity process with the oldest being 8 years old. They are also relatively vertical specific: SIF is primarily pK-12, LOM is primarily Corp, Military and Higher Ed, and SCORM is primarily Military and Corp with some Higher Ed. PESC— the Post-Secondary Education Standards Council— is also making headway in developing standards and learning objects for the Higher Ed space, while SIF is beginning to seriously turn towards Instructional and Curriculum learning objects.

In the US pK12 space there are a host of content standards that are critical as well- the NCES data standards are a prime example. Each state government's content standards and achievement benchmarks are critical metadata for linking e-learning objects in that space.

An excellent example of e-learning that relates to knowledge management and reusability is Navy E-Learning, which is available to Active Duty, Retired, or Disable Military members. This on-line tool provides certificate courses to enrich the user in various subjects related to military training and civilian skill sets. The e-learning system not only provides learning objectives, but also evaluates the progress of the student and credit can be earned toward higher learning institutions. This reuse is an excellent example of knowledge retention and the cyclical process of knowledge transfer and use of data and records.

4
Learning Management System

A learning management system (LMS) is a software application for the administration, documentation, tracking, and reporting of training programmes, classroom and online events, e-learning programs, and training content.

LMSs range from systems for managing training and educational records, to software for distributing courses over the Internet with features for online collaboration. Corporate training use LMSs to automate record-keeping and employee registration. Student self-service (e.g., self-registration on instructor-led training), training workflow (e.g., user notification, manager approval, wait-list management), the provision of on-line learning (e.g., Computer-Based Training, read & understand), on-line assessment, management of continuous professional education (CPE), collaborative learning (e.g., application sharing, discussion threads), and training resource management (e.g., instructors, facilities, equipment), are dimensions to Learning Management Systems.

Some LMSs are Web-based to facilitate access to learning content and administration. LMSs are used by regulated industries (e.g. financial services and biopharma) for compliance training. It is also used by educational institutions to enhance and support classroom teaching and offering courses to a larger population of learners across the globe.

Some LMS providers include "performance management systems", which encompass employee appraisals, competency management, skills-gap analysis, succession planning, and multi-rater assessments (i.e., 360 degree reviews).

For the commercial market, some Learning and Performance Management Systems include recruitment and reward functionality.

Characteristics

LMSs cater to educational, administrative, and deployment requirements. While an LMS for corporate learning, for example, may share many characteristics with a VLE, or virtual learning environment, used by educational institutions, they each meet unique needs. The virtual learning environment used by universities and colleges allow instructors to manage their courses and exchange information with students for a course that in most cases will last several weeks and will meet several times during those weeks. In the corporate setting a course may be much shorter, completed in a single instructor-led or online session.

The characteristics shared by both types of LMSs include:

- Manage users, roles, courses, instructors, facilities, and generate reports
- Course calendar
- Learning Path
- Student messaging and notifications
- Assessment and testing handling before and after testing
- Display scores and transcripts
- Grading of coursework and roster processing, including waitlisting
- Web-based or blended course delivery

Characteristics more specific to corporate learning, which sometimes includes franchisees or other business partners, include:

- Autoenrollment (enrolling Students in courses when required according to predefined criteria, such as job title or work location)
- Manager enrollment and approval
- Boolean definitions for prerequisites or equivalencies
- Integration with performance tracking and management systems
- Planning tools to identify skill gaps at departmental and individual level
- Curriculum, required and elective training requirements at an individual and organizational level
- Grouping students according to demographic units (geographic region, product line, business size, etc.)
- Assign corporate and partner employees to more than one job title at more than one demographic unit

Technical Aspects

LMSs are based on a variety of development platforms, like Java/J2EE based architectures, Microsoft .NET, PHP, and usually employ the use of a database as back-end. Some systems are commercially developed and have non-free software licenses or restrict access to their source code, Other systems are free and open-source and frequently used. Other than the most simple, basic functionality, LMSs cater to, and focus on, different educational, administrative, and deployment requirements.

Learning Content Management System (LCMS)

A learning content management system (LCMS) is a related technology to the learning management system (*e.g.*, Murray Goldberg's WebCT), in that it is focused on the development, management and publishing of the content that will typically be delivered via an LMS. An LCMS is a multi-user environment where developers may create, store, **reuse**, manage, and deliver digital learning content from a central object repository. The LMS cannot create and manipulate courses; it cannot reuse the content of one course to build another. The LCMS, however, can create, manage and deliver not only training modules but also manage and edit all the individual pieces that make up a catalog of training. LCMS applications allow users to create, import, manage, search for and reuse small units or "chunks" of digital learning content and assets, commonly referred to as learning objects. These assets may include media files developed in other authoring tools, assessment items, simulations, text, graphics or any other object that makes up the content within the course being created. An LCMS manages the process of creating, editing, storing and delivering e-learning content, ILT materials and other training support deliverables such as job aids.

Learning Management Systems compared to Learning Content Management Systems

Some systems have tools to deliver and manage instructor-led synchronous and asynchronous online training based on learning object methodology. These systems are called Learning Content Management Systems or LCMSs. LCMSs provide tools for authoring and reusing or re-purposing content (mutated learning objects) MLO as well as virtual spaces for student interaction (such as discussion forums, live chat rooms and live web-conferences). Despite this distinction, the term LMS is often used to refer to both an LMS and an LCMS, although the LCMS is a further development of the LMS. Due to this conformity issue, the acronym Clcims (*Computer Learning Content Information Management System*) is now widely used to create a uniform phonetic way of referencing any learning system software based on advanced learning technology methodology.

In essence, an LMS is software for planning, delivering, and managing learning events within an organization, including online, virtual classroom, and instructor-led courses. For example, an LMS can simplify global certification efforts, enable entities to align learning initiatives with strategic goals, and provide a means of enterprise-level skills management. The focus of an LMS is to manage students, keeping track of their progress and performance across all types of training activities. It performs administrative tasks, such as reporting to instructors, HR and other ERP systems but isn't used to create course content.

In contrast, an LCMS is software for managing learning content across an organization's various training development areas. It provides developers, authors, instructional designers, and subject matter experts the means to create and re-use e-learning content and reduce duplicated development efforts. In the remote AICC hosting approach, an LCMS may host the content in a central repository and allow multiple LMSs to access it.

Primary business problems an LCMS solves are

- centralized management of an organization's learning content for efficient searching and retrieval,
- productivity gains around rapid and condensed development timelines,
- productivity gains around assembly, maintenance and publishing / branding / delivery of learning content.

Rather than developing entire courses and adapting them to multiple audiences, an LCMS provides the ability for single course instances to be modified and republished for various audiences maintaining versions and history. The objects stored in the centralized repository can be made available to course developers and content experts throughout an organization for potential reuse and repurpose. This eliminates duplicate development efforts and allows for the rapid assembly of customized content.

Learning Management Industry

In the relatively new LMS market, commercial vendors for corporate and education applications range from new entrants to those that entered the market in the nineties. In addition to commercial packages, many open source solutions are available.

In 2009, LMSs represented an $860 million market, made up of more than 60 different providers. The six largest LMS product companies constitute approximately 50% of the market (Bersin et al. 2009). In addition to the remaining smaller LMS product vendors, training outsourcing firms, enterprise resource planning vendors, and consulting firms all compete for part of the learning management market.

LMS buyers generally report poor satisfaction based on survey results from the American Society for Training and Development (ASTD) and the eLearningGuild. The ASTD respondents who were very unsatisfied with an LMS purchase doubled, and those that were very satisfied decreased by 25%. The number that were very satisfied or satisfied edged over 50%. (About 30% were somewhat satisfied.) Nearly one quarter of respondents intended to purchase a new LMS or outsource their LMS functionality over the next 12 months. eLearningGuild respondents report significant barriers including cost, IT support, integration, and customization. They also report significant effort to implement with a median of 23 months being reported from requirements gathering to implementation for corporations with more than 2,000 employees.

Channel learning is under-served. For many buyers channel learning is not their number one priority, according to a survey by Trainingindustry.com (Expertus & TrainingOutsourcing 2006). Often there is a disconnect when the HR department oversees training and development initiatives, where the focus is consolidating LMS systems inside traditional corporate boundaries. Software technology companies are at the front end of this curve, placing higher priority on channel training.

Today the biggest trend in the LMS market is for these systems to be integrated with "Talent Management" software systems. The largest LMS providers have performance management, collaborative learning, content management, succession management, and other talent management modules to their systems. Bersin research shows that in 2009 more than 70% of large companies have an LMS already and almost 1/3 of these companies are considering replacing or upgrading these systems with integrated talent management systems.

Most buyers of LMSs utilize an authoring tool to create their e-learning content, which is then hosted on an LMS. Buyers, however, must choose an authoring software that integrates with their LMS in order for their content to be hosted. There are authoring tools on the market, which meet AICC and SCORM standards and therefore content created in tools such as these can be hosted on an AICC or SCORM certified LMS.

LEARNING OBJECT

A **learning object** is a resource, usually digital and web-based, that can be used and re-used to support learning.

Learning objects offer a new conceptualization of the learning process: rather than the traditional "several hour chunk", they provide smaller, self-contained, re-usable units of learning.

They will typically have a number of different components, which range from descriptive data to information about rights and educational level. At their core, however, will be instructional content, practice, and assessment. A key issue is the use of metadata.

Learning object design raises issues of portability, and of the object's relation to a broader learning management system.

Definitions

There are various definitions of the term. As David Wiley observes, "the proliferation of definitions for the term 'learning object' makes communication confusing and difficult".

Most generally, the Institute of Electrical and Electronics Engineers (IEEE) defines a learning object as "any entity, digital or non-digital, that may be used for learning, education or training". More specifically, and pointing out the extreme breadth of the IEEE's definition, Wiley describes a learning object as "any *digital* resource that can be *re*used to support learning".

Chiappe defined Learning Objects as: "A digital self-contained and reusable entity, with a clear educational purpose, with at least three internal and editable components: content, learning activities and elements of context. The learning objects must have an external structure of information to facilitate their identification, storage and retrieval: the metadata."

The following definitions focus on the relation between learning object and digital media. RLO-CETL, a British inter-university Learning Objects Center, defines "reusable learning objects" as "web-based interactive chunks of e-learning designed to explain a stand-alone learning objective". Daniel Rehak and Robin Mason define it as "a digitized entity which can be used, reused or referenced during technology supported learning".

Adapting a definition from the Wisconsin Online Resource Center, Robert J. Beck suggests that learning objects have the following key characteristics:

- Learning objects are a new way of thinking about learning content. Traditionally, content comes in a several hour chunk. Learning objects are much smaller units of learning, typically ranging from 2 minutes to 15 minutes.
- Are self-contained – each learning object can be taken independently.
- Are reusable – a single learning object may be used in multiple contexts for multiple purposes.
- Can be aggregated – learning objects can be grouped into larger collections of content, including traditional course structures.
- Are tagged with metadata – every learning object has descriptive information allowing it to be easily found by a search.

Components

The following is a list of some of the types of information that may be included in a learning object and its metadata:

- General Course Descriptive Data, including: course identifiers, language of content (English, Spanish, etc.), subject area (Maths, Reading, etc.), descriptive text, descriptive keywords.
- Life Cycle, including: version, status.
- Instructional Content, including: text, web pages, images, sound, video.
- Glossary of Terms, including: terms, definition, acronyms.

- Quizzes and Assessments, including: questions, answers.
- Rights, including: cost, copyrights, restrictions on Use.
- Relationships to Other Courses, including prerequisite courses.
- Educational Level, including: grade level, age range, typical learning time, and difficulty. [IEEE 1484.12.1:2002].

Metadata

One of the key issues in using learning objects is their identification by search engines. This is usually facilitated by assigning descriptive learning object metadata. Just as a book in a library has a record in the card catalog, learning objects must also be tagged with metadata.

Mutability

A mutated learning object is, according to Michael Shaw, a learning object that has been "re-purposed and/or re-engineered, changed or simply re-used in some way different from its original intended design". Shaw also introduces the term "contextual learning object", to describe a learning object that has been "designed to have specific meaning and purpose to an intended learner".

Portability

Before any institution invests a great deal of time and energy into building high-quality e-learning content (which can cost over $10,000 per classroom hour), it needs to consider how this content can be easily loaded into a Learning Management System. It is possible for example, to package learning objects with SCORM specification and load it at Moodle Learning Management System.

If all of the properties of a course can be precisely defined in a common format, the content can be serialized into a standard format such as XML and loaded into other systems. When you consider that some e-learning courses need to include video, mathematical equations using MathML, chemistry equations using CML and other complex structures the issues become very complex, especially if the systems needs to understand and validate each structure and then place it correctly in a database.

Learning Object Projects

Some examples of learning object projects include:

- AGORA, a publicly accessible online learning environment at the Virtual Museum of Canada. Content is created and produced by Canadian museum educators.
- eduSource, a Canada-wide project to create the infrastructure for a network of inter-operable learning object repositories. The eduSource project is based on national and international standards; it is bilingual (French and English) and designed to be fully accessible.
- MERLOT (Multimedia Educational Resource for Learning and Online Teaching), a free and open resource designed primarily for faculty and students of higher education.
- IQity Reactor is a learning object repository that allows educators to create and share custom curriculum, organized by state educational standards. Reactor is integrated with a learning management system.
- Wisc-Online is a web-based repository of learning objects, developed primarily by faculty members from the Wisconsin Technical College System.

LEARNING OBJECT METADATA

Learning Object Metadata is a data model, usually encoded in XML, used to describe a learning object and similar digital resources used to support learning. The purpose of learning object metadata is to support the reusability of learning objects, to aid discoverability, and to facilitate their interoperability, usually in the context of online learning management systems (LMS).

The IEEE 1484.12.1 – 2002 Standard for Learning Object Metadata is an internationally-recognised open standard (published by the Institute of Electrical and Electronics Engineers Standards Association, New York) for the description of "learning objects". Relevant attributes of learning objects to be described include: type of object; author; owner; terms of distribution; format; and pedagogical attributes, such as teaching or interaction style.

IEEE 1484.12.1 – 2002 Standard for Learning Object Metadata

In brief

The IEEE working group that developed the standard defined learning objects, *for the purposes of the standard,* as being "any entity, digital or non-digital, that may be used for learning, education or training." This definition has struck many commentators as being rather broad in its scope, but it should be noted that the definition was intended to provide a broad class of objects to which LOM metadata might usefully be associated rather than to give an instructional or pedagogic definition of a learning object. *IEEE 1484.12.1* is the first part of a multipart standard, and describes the LOM data model. The LOM data model specifies which aspects of a learning object should be described and what vocabularies may be used for these descriptions; it also defines how this data model can be amended by additions or constraints. Other parts of the standard are being drafted to define bindings of the LOM data model, i.e. define how LOM records should be represented in XML and RDF (*IEEE 1484.12.3* and *IEEE 1484.12.4* respectively). This article focuses on the LOM data model rather than issues relating to XML or other bindings.

IMS Global Learning Consortium is an international consortium that contributed to the drafting of the IEEE Learning Object Metadata (together with the ARIADNE Foundation) and endorsed early drafts of the data model as part of the IMS Learning Resource Meta-data specification (IMS LRM, versions 1.0 – 1.2.2). Feedback and suggestions from the implementers of IMS LRM fed into the further development of the LOM, resulting in some drift between version 1.2 of the IMS LRM specification and what was finally published at the LOM standard. Version 1.3 of the IMS LRM specification realigns the IMS LRM data model with the IEEE LOM data model and specifies that the IEEE XML binding should be used. Thus, we can now use the term 'LOM' in referring to both the IEEE standard and version 1.3 of the IMS specification. The IMS LRM specification also provides an extensive *Best Practice and Implementation Guide*, and an *XSL transform* that can be used to migrate metadata instances from the older versions of the IMS LRM XML binding to the IEEE LOM XML binding.

Technical Details

How the Data Model Works?

The LOM comprises a **hierarchy of elements**. At the first level, there are nine categories, each of which contains sub-elements; these sub-elements may be simple elements that hold data, or may themselves be aggregate elements, which contain further sub-elements. The semantics of an element are determined by its context: they are affected by the parent or container element in the hierarchy and by other elements in the same container. For example, the various *Description* elements (1.4, 5.10, 6.3, 7.2.2, 8.3 and 9.3) each derive their context from their parent element. In addition, description element 9.3 also takes its context from the value of element 9.1 *Purpose* in the same instance of *Classification*.

The data model specifies that some elements may be repeated either individually or as a group; for example, although the elements 9.3 (*Description*) and 9.1 (*Purpose*) can only occur once within each instance of the *Classification* container element, the *Classification* element may be repeated — thus allowing many descriptions for different purposes.

The data model also specifies the **value space** and **datatype** for each of the simple data elements. The value space defines the restrictions, if any, on the data that can be entered for that element. For many elements, the value space allows any string of Unicode character to be entered, whereas other elements entries must be drawn from a declared list (i.e. a controlled vocabulary) or must be in a specified format (e.g. date and language codes). Some element datatypes simply allow a string of characters to be entered, and others comprise two parts, as described below:

- **LangString** items contain Language and String parts, allowing the same information to be recorded in multiple languages.
- **Vocabulary** items are constrained in such a way that their entries have to be chosen from a controlled list of terms - composed of Source-Value pairs - with the Source containing the name of the list of terms being used and the Value containing the chosen term.
- **DateTime** and **Duration** items contain one part that allows the date or duration to be given in a machine readable format, and a second that allows a description of the date or duration (for example "mid summer, 1968").

When implementing the LOM as a data or service provider, it is not necessary to support all the elements in the data model, nor need the LOM data model limit the information which may be provided. The creation of an application profile allows a community of users to specify which elements and vocabularies they will use. Elements from the LOM may be dropped and elements from other metadata schemas may be brought in; likewise, the vocabularies in the LOM may be supplemented with values appropriate to that community.

Requirements

The key requirements for exploiting the LOM as a data or service provider are to:

- Understand user/community needs and to express these as an application profile
- Have a strategy for creating high quality metadata
- Store this metadata in a form which can be exported as LOM records
- Agree a binding for LOM instances when they are exchanged
- Be able to exchange records with other systems either as single instances or *en masse*.

Related Specifications

There are many metadata specifications; of particular interest is the Dublin Core Metadata Element Set (commonly known as Simple Dublin Core, standardised as *ANSI/NISO Z39.85 – 2001*), which provides a simpler, more loosely-defined set of elements with some overlap with the LOM, and which is useful for sharing metadata across a wide range of disparate services. The Dublin Core Metadata Initiative is also working on a set of terms which allow the Dublin Core Element Set to be used with greater semantic precision (Qualified Dublin

Core). The Dublin Education Working Group aims to provide refinements of Dublin Core for the specific needs of the education community. Details of Dublin Core can be found at the Dublin Core website.

Many other education-related specifications allow for LO metadata to be embedded within XML instances, such as: describing the resources in an IMS Content Package or Resource List; describing the vocabularies and terms in an IMS VDEX (Vocabulary Definition and Exchange) file; and describing the question items in an IMS QTI (Question and Test Interoperability) file. Details of these can be found at the IMS Global website.

The IMS Vocabulary Definition and Exchange (VDEX) specification has a double relation with the LOM, since not only can the LOM provide metadata on the vocabularies in a VDEX instance, but VDEX can be used to describe the controlled vocabularies which are the value space for many LOM elements.

LOM records can be transported between systems using a variety of protocols, perhaps the most widely used being OAI-PMH.

Application Profiles

UK LOM Core

For UK Further and Higher Education, the most relevant family of application profiles are those based around the *UK LOM Core* . The UK LOM Core is currently a draft schema researched by a community of practitioners to identify common UK practice in learning object content, by comparing 12 metadata schemas.

Can Core

Can Core provides detailed guidance for the interpretation and implementation of each data element in the LOM standard.

These guidelines constitute a 250-page document, and have been developed over three years under the leadership of Norm Friesen, and through consultation with experts across Canada and throughout the world. These guidelines are also available at no charge from the CanCore Website.

ANZ-LOM

ANZ-LOM is a metadata profile developed for the education sector in Australia and New Zealand. The profile provides interpretations of metadata structures and illustrates how to apply controlled vocabularies, especially using the "classification" element.

It is supported by detailed examples of learning resource metadata, including regional vocabularies. The ANZ-LOM profile was first published by The Learning Federation (TLF) in January, 2008.

Vetadata

The Australian Vocational Training and Education (VET) sector uses an application profile of the IEEE LOM called Vetadata. The profile contains five mandatory elements, and makes use of a number of vocabularies specific to the Australian VET sector. This application profile was first published in 2005. The Vetadata and ANZ-LOM profiles are closely aligned.

NORLOM

NORLOM is the Norwegian LOM profile. The profile is managed by NSSL (The Norwegian Secretariat for Standardization of Learning Technologies)

ISRACore

ISRACORE is the Israeli LOM profile. The Israel Internet Association (ISOC-IL) and Inter University Computational Center (IUCC) have teamed up to manage and establish an e-learning objects database.

Others

Other important application profiles are those developed by the Celebrate project and the metadata profile that is part of the SCORM reference model.

Learning Pathway

The chosen route, taken by a learner through a range of (commonly) e-learning activities, which allows them to build knowledge progressively. With learning pathways, the control of choice moves away from the tutor to the learner. "The sequence of intermediate steps from preconceptions to target model form what Scott and Niedderer and Goldberg have called a learning pathway. For any particular topic, such a pathway would provide both a theory of instruction and a guideline for teachers and curriculum developers".

"Interactive courseware aids learners to access information and tools by which they can construct personalized transitions between the information to be accessed and their own cognitive structures. The process of navigation enables learners to experience the content of interactive courseware. Learning pathways also reveal the learning trails while learners traverse any interactive environment. Since learners have unique knowledge structures based upon their experiences and abilities, the ways that they choose to access, interact, and interrelate messages in interactive courseware also vary. Studies on pathways help us to explore and explain human behaviors during learning processes".

Lesson Study

Lesson Study (or *kenkyu jugyo*) is a teaching improvement process that has origins in Japanese elementary education, where it is a widespread professional development practice. Working in a small group, teachers collaborate with one another, meeting to discuss learning goals, to plan an actual classroom lesson (called a "research lesson"), to observe how it works in practice, and then to revise and report on the results so that other teachers can benefit from it. Despite differences between Japanese and American educational systems, the practice is gaining in popularity in the United States in K-12 education and teacher training, and more recently it is finding a home in higher education as a form of faculty development.

This is a specific example of the on-going Japanese devotion to the Plan-Do-Check-Act PDCA decision-making discipline pioneered by W. Edwards Deming, which is based upon the Shewhart Cycle (named after Deming's collaborator from Bell Telephone Laboratories, Walter A. Shewhart).

●●

5
Microlearning

Microlearning deals with relatively small learning units and short-term learning activities. Generally, the term 'microlearning' refers to micro-perspectives in the context of learning, education and training. More frequently, the term is used in the domain of E-learning and related fields in the sense of a new paradigmatic perspective on learning processes in mediated environments on micro levels.

In a wide sense, microlearning can be understood as a metaphor which refers to micro aspects of a variety of learning models, concepts and processes.

"No matter if learning refers to the process of building up and organizing knowledge, to the change of behaviour, of attitudes, of values, of mental abilities, of cognitive structures, of emotional reactions, of action patterns or of societal dimensions, in all cases we have the possibility to consider micro, meso and macro aspects of the various views on more or less persisting changes and sustainable alterations of performances."

Depending on frames and domains of reference, micro, meso and macro aspects vary. They are relational concepts. For example, in the context of language learning, one might think of micro aspects in terms of vocabularies, phrases, sentences, and distinguish them from situations and episodes (meso aspects) and socio-cultural specifics or complex semantics (macro aspects). In a more general discourse on learning, one might differentiate between the learning of individuals, group learning or learning of organizations and the learning of generations or societies.

Furthermore, microlearning marks a transition from common models of learning towards micro perspectives on and the significance of micro dimensions in the process of learning. The microlearning approach is an emergent paradigm, so there are no hard definitions or coherent uses of the term yet. However, the growing focus on microlearning activities can be seen by web users' activities on the subject, who tag their corresponding weblog postings and social bookmarks with the term 'microlearning' (check the corresponding Technorati and del.icio.us tags for examples).

As an instructional technology, microlearning focuses on the design of micro learning activities through micro steps in digital media environments, which already is a daily reality for today's knowledge workers. These activities can be incorporated in learner's daily routines and tasks. Unlike "traditional" elearning approaches, microlearning often tends towards push technology through push media, which reduces the cognitive load on the learners. Therefore, the selection of micro learning objects and also pace and timing of micro learning activities are of importance for didactical designs.

Characterization of Microlearning

Microlearning can be characterized as follows:

- Microlearning processes often derive from interaction with microcontent, which takes place either in designed (media) settings (eLearning) or in emergent microcontent structures like weblog postings or social bookmark managers on the World Wide Web.
- Microlearning can be an assumption about the time needed to solve a learning task, for example answering a question, memorizing an information item, or finding a needed resource. Learning processes that have

been called "microlearning" can cover a span from few seconds (e.g. in mobile learning) up to 15 minutes or more. There is some relation to the term microteaching, which is an established practice in teacher education.

- Microlearning can also be understood as a *process* of subsequent, "short" learning activities, i.e. learning through interaction with microcontent objects in small timeframes. In this case, the design, selection, feedback and pacing of repeated or otherwise 'chained' microlearning tasks comes into view.
- In a wider sense, microlearning is a term that can be used to describe the way more and more people are actually doing informal learning and gaining knowledge in microcontent, micromedia or multitasking environments (microcosm), especially those that become increasingly based on Web 2.0 and wireless web technologies. In this wider sense, the borders between microlearning and the complementary concept of microknowledge are blurring.

Dimensions of Microlearning

The following dimensions can be used to describe or design micro learning activities:

- **Time:** Relatively short effort, operating expense, degree of time consumption, measurable time, subjective time, etc.
- **Content:** Small or very small units, narrow topics, rather simple issues, etc.
- **Curriculum:** Small part of curricular setting, parts of modules, elements of informal learning, etc.
- **Form:** Fragments, facets, episodes, "knowledge nuggets", skill elements, etc.

- **Process:** Separate, concomitant or actual, situated or integrated activities, iterative method, attention management, awareness (getting into or being in a process), etc.
- **Mediality:** Print media, electronic media, mono-media vs. multi-media, (inter-)mediated forms, etc.
- **Learning type:** Repetitive, activist, reflective, pragmatist, conceptionalist, constructivist, connectivist, behaviourist; also: action learning, classroom learning, corporate learning, etc.

Examples of Microlearning Activities

- reading a paragraph of text, email or sms
- listening to an informational (short) podcast or an educational video-clip
- viewing a flashcard
- memorizing a word, vocabulary, definition or formula
- sorting a set of (microcontent) items by (chrono)logical order
- selecting an answer to a question
- answering questions in quizzes
- playful learning with micro-games
- composing a haiku or a short poem

Microlearning Applications (Examples)

- Screensavers which prompt the user to solve small series of simple tasks after a certain amount of inactivity
- Quizzes with multiple choice options on cell phones by use of sms or mobile applications (java midlets, symbian)
- Word of the day as daily RSS-feed or email

- Flashcard-software for memorizing content through spaced repetition

MICROLECTURE

The term **microlecture** is used not to refer to microcontent for microlearning, but to actual instructional content that is formatted for online and mobile learning using a constructivist approach. More specifically, as described in the Chronicle of Higher Education , these are approximately 60 second presentations with a specific structure. They are not just brief (one minute) presentations: although Dr. McGrew had success with "one minute lectures" at the University of Northern Iowa as did Dr. Kee at the University of Leeds.

David M. Penrose (aka the One Minute Professor), the Senior Instructional Designer and Manager of Online Services at San Juan College, of SunGard Higher Education has articulated the process for creating these **microlectures**. As stated (Shieh, 2009), these specific lectures are combined with specific activities designed to promote the epistemic engagement of the learner. The response of the Higher Education community was mixed, with some positive and some negative.

How to Create a One Minute Lecture?

Professors spend a lot of time crafting hourlong lectures. The prospect of boiling them down to 60 seconds — or even five minutes — may seem daunting. David Penrose, a course designer for SunGard Higher Education who developed San Juan College's microlectures, suggests that it can be done in five steps:

- List the key concepts you are trying to convey in the 60-minute lecture.

That series of phrases will form the core of your microlecture.

- Write a 15 to 30-second introduction and conclusion.

They will provide context for your key concepts.

- Record these three elements using a microphone and Web camera.

If you want to produce an audio-only lecture, no Webcam is necessary.

The finished product should be 60 seconds to three minutes long.

- Design an assignment to follow the lecture that will direct students to readings or activities that allow them to explore the key concepts.

Combined with a written assignment, that should allow students to learn the material.

- Upload the video and assignment to your course-management software.

MIND MAP

A **mind map** is a diagram used to represent words, ideas, tasks, or other items linked to and arranged around a central key word or idea. Mind maps are used to generate, visualize, structure, and classify ideas, and as an aid in study, organization, problem solving, decision making, and writing.

The elements of a given mind map are arranged intuitively according to the importance of the concepts, and are classified into groupings, branches, or areas, with the goal of representing semantic or other connections between portions of information. Mind maps may also aid recall of existing memories.

By presenting ideas in a radial, graphical, non-linear manner, mind maps encourage a brainstorming approach to planning and organizational tasks. Though the branches of a mindmap represent hierarchical tree structures, their radial arrangement disrupts the prioritizing of concepts typically associated with hierarchies presented with more linear visual cues. This orientation towards brainstorming encourages users to enumerate and connect concepts without a tendency to begin within a particular conceptual framework.

The mind map can be contrasted with the similar idea of concept mapping. The former is based on radial hierarchies and tree structures denoting relationships with a central governing concept, whereas concept maps are based on connections between concepts in more diverse patterns.

An industry standard that implements formal rules for finalizing at least a subset of such diagrams is the Unified Modeling Language (UML).

Characteristics

Mind maps are, by definition, a graphical method of taking notes. The visual basis of them helps one to distinguish words or ideas, often with colors and symbols. They generally take a hierarchical or tree branch format, with ideas branching into their subsections. Mind maps allow for greater creativity when recording ideas and information, as well as allowing the note-taker to associate words with visual representations. Mind maps and concept maps are different in that mind maps focus on *only* one word or idea, whereas Concept maps connect multiple words or ideas.

Mind maps (or similar concepts) have been used for centuries in learning, brainstorming, memory, visual thinking, and problem solving by educators, engineers, psychologists, and others. Some of the earliest examples of mind maps were developed by Porphyry of Tyros, a noted thinker of the 3rd century, as he graphically visualized the concept categories of Aristotle. Philosopher Ramon Llull (1235 - 1315) also used mind maps.

The semantic network was developed in the late 1950s as a theory to understand human learning and developed into mind maps by Allan M. Collins and M. Ross Quillian during the early 1960s. Due to his commitment and published research, and his work with learning, creativity, and graphical thinking, Collins can be considered the father of the modern mind map.

British popular psychology author Tony Buzan claims to have invented modern mind mapping. He claimed the idea was inspired by Alfred Korzybski's general semantics as popularized in science fiction novels, such as those of Robert A. Heinlein and A. E. van Vogt. Buzan argues that while 'traditional' outlines force readers to scan left to right and top to bottom, readers actually tend to scan the entire page in a non-linear fashion. Buzan also uses popular assumptions about the cerebral hemispheres in order to promote the exclusive use of mind mapping over other forms of note making.

The mind map continues to be used in various forms, and for various applications including learning and education (where it is often taught as 'Webs', 'Mind webs', or 'Webbing'), planning, and in engineering diagramming.

When compared with the concept map (which was developed by learning experts in the 1970s) the structure of a mind map is a similar radial, but is simplified by having one central key word.

Uses

A mind map is often created around a single word or text, placed in the center, to which associated ideas, words and concepts are added.

Mind maps have many applications in personal, family, educational, and business situations, including notetaking, brainstorming (wherein ideas are inserted into the map radially around the center node, without the implicit prioritization that comes from hierarchy or sequential arrangements, and wherein grouping and organizing is reserved for later stages), summarizing, revising, and general clarifying of thoughts. One could listen to a lecture, for example, and take down notes using mind maps for the most important points or keywords. One can also use mind maps as a mnemonic technique or to sort out a complicated idea. Mind maps are also promoted as a way to collaborate in color pen creativity sessions.

Mind maps can be used for:

- Problem Solving.
- Outline / Framework Design.
- Anonymous collaboration.
- Marriage of words and visuals.
- Individual expression of creativity.
- Condensing material into a concise and memorable format.
- Team building or synergy creating activity.
- Enhancing work morale.

Mindmaps can be drawn by hand, either as 'rough notes' during a lecture or meeting, for example, or can be more sophisticated in quality. Examples of both are illustrated. There are also a number of software packages available for producing mind maps.

Effectiveness in Learning

Buzan claims that the mind map is a vastly superior note taking method because it does not lead to a "semi-hypnotic trance" state induced by other note forms. Buzan also argues that the mind map uses the full range of left and right human cortical skills, balances the brain, taps into the apocryphal 99% of your unused mental potential, as well as intuition (which he calls "superlogic"). However, scholarly research suggests that such claims may actually be marketing hype based on misconceptions about the brain and the cerebral hemispheres. Critics argue that hemispheric specialization theory has been identified as pseudoscientific when applied to mind mapping.

Scholarly research by Farrand, Hussain, and Hennessy found that the mind map technique had a limited but significant impact on memory recall in undergraduate students (a 10% increase over baseline for a 600-word text only) as compared to preferred study methods (a "6% increase over baseline). This improvement was only robust after a week for those in the mind map group (actually it was 'spider diagrams' not Mind Maps used in this study) and there was a significant decrease in motivation compared to the subjects' preferred methods of note taking. Farrand *et al.* suggested that learners preferred to use other methods because using a mind map was an unfamiliar technique, and its status as a "memory enhancing" technique engendered reluctance to apply it. Nevertheless the conclusion of the study was "Mind maps provide an effective study technique when applied to written material. However before mind maps are generally adopted as a study technique, consideration has to be given towards ways of improving motivation amongst users."

Pressley, VanEtten, Yokoi, Freebern, and VanMeter found that learners tended to learn far better by focusing on the content of learning material rather than worrying over any one particular form of note taking.

Tools

Mind mapping software can be used effectively to organize large amounts of information, combining spatial organization, dynamic hierarchical structuring and node folding. Software packages can extend the concept of mind mapping by allowing individuals to map more than thoughts and ideas with information on their computers and the internet, like spreadsheets, documents, internet sites and images.

Trademarks

The use of the term "Mind Maps" is claimed as a trademark by The Buzan Organisation, Ltd. in the UK and the USA. The trade-mark does not appear in the records of the Canadian Intellectual Property Office. In the U.S. "Mind Maps" is trademarked as a "service mark" expressly for "EDUCATIONAL SERVICES, NAMELY, CONDUCTING COURSES IN SELF-IMPROVEMENT" – other products and services are not covered by the trademark.

MINIMALLY INVASIVE EDUCATION

Minimally Invasive Education (or **MIE**) is a term used to describe how children learn in unsupervised environments. It was derived from an experiment done by Sugata Mitra while at NIIT in 1999 often called *The Hole in the Wall*.

It has since gone on to become a significant project with the formation of Hole in the Wall Education Limited (HiWEL), a cooperative effort between NIIT and the International Finance Corporation, employed in some 300 'learning stations', covering some 300,000 children in India and several African countries.

The programme has been feted with the digital opportunity award by WITSA, and been extensively covered in the media.

Background

Dr. Sugata Mitra, Chief Scientist at NIIT, is credited with proposing and initiating the Hole-in-the-Wall programme. As early as 1982, he had been toying with the idea of unsupervised learning and computers. Finally, in 1999, he decided to test his ideas in the field.

The Experiment

On 26 January, 1999, Dr. Mitra's team carved a "hole in the wall" that separated the NIIT premises from the adjoining slum in Kalkaji, New Delhi. Through this hole, a freely accessible computer was put up for use. This computer proved to be popular among the slum children. With no prior experience, the children learnt to use the computer on their own. This prompted Dr. Mitra to propose the following hypothesis:

The acquisition of basic computing skills by any set of children can be achieved through incidental learning provided the learners are given access to a suitable computing facility, with entertaining and motivating content and some minimal (human) guidance.

Results and Expansion

The first adopter of the idea was the Government of National Capital Territory of Delhi. In 2000, the Government of Delhi set up 30 Learning Stations in a resettlement colony. This project is ongoing and said to be achieving significant results.

Encouraged by the initial success of the Kalkaji experiment, freely accessible computers were set up in Shivpuri (a town in Madhya Pradesh) and in Madantusi (a village in Uttar Pradesh). These experiments came to be known as Hole-in-the-Wall experiments. The findings from Shivpuri and Madantusi confirmed the results of Kalkaji experiments. It appeared that the children in these two places picked up computer skills on their own. Dr. Mitra defined this as a new way of learning "Minimally Invasive Education".

At this point in time, International Finance Corporation joined hands with NIIT to set up Hole-in-the-Wall Education Ltd (HiWEL). The idea was to broaden the scope of the experiments and conduct research to prove and streamline Hole-in-the-Wall. The results, show that children learn to operate as well as play with the computer with minimum intervention. They picked up skills and tasks by constructing their own learning environment.

Current Status and Expansion Outside India

Today, more than 300,000 children have benefited from 300 Hole-in-the-Wall stations over last 8 years. The number is going to double with more than 200 stations being installed in 2009.

Besides India, HiWEL also has projects abroad. The first such project was established in Cambodia in 2004. The project currently operates in Botswana, Mozambique, Nigeria, Rwanda, Swaziland, Uganda, and Zambia, besides Cambodia.

HiWEL

Hole-in-the-Wall Education Ltd. (HiWEL) is a joint venture between NIIT and the International Finance Corporation. Established in 2001, HiWEL was set up to research and propagate the idea of Hole-in-the-Wall, a path-breaking learning methodology created by Dr. Sugata Mitra, Chief Scientist of NIIT.

Awards and Recognition

Digital Opportunity Award by the World Information Technology and Services Alliance (WITSA) in 2008. Reason: "groundbreaking work in developing computer literacy and improving the quality of education at a grass root level."

Coverage in the Media

The project has received extensive coverage from sources as diverse as UNESCO, Business Week, CNN, Reuters, and The Christian Science Monitor; besides being featured at the annual TED conference in 2007.

The project received international publicity, when it was found that it was the inspiration behind the book Q & A (novel), itself the inspiration for the Academy Award winning film Slumdog Millionaire.

mLEARNING

The term **mLearning**, or "mobile learning", has different meanings for different communities. Although related to e-learning and distance education, it is distinct in its focus on learning across contexts and learning with mobile devices. One definition of mobile learning is: *Any sort of learning that happens when the learner is not at a fixed, predetermined location, or learning that happens when the learner takes advantage of the learning opportunities offered by mobile technologies.* In other words, mobile learning decreases limitation of learning location with the mobility of general portable devices.

The term covers: learning with portable technologies, where the focus is on the technology (which could be in a fixed location, such as a classroom); learning across contexts, where the focus is on the mobility of the learner, interacting with portable or fixed technology; and learning in a mobile society, with a focus on how society and its institutions can accommodate and support the learning of an increasingly mobile population that is not satisfied with existing learning methodologies.

M-learning is convenient in the sense that it is accessible from virtually anywhere, which provides access to all the different learning materials available. It is also collaborative; sharing is almost instantaneous among everyone using the same content, which leads to the reception of instant feedback and tips. M-Learning also brings strong portability by replacing books and notes with small RAMs, filled with tailored learning contents. In addition, this kind of learning is engaging and fun. Therefore, it is simple to utilize mobile learning for a more effective and entertaining experience.

1970s and 1980s

Alan Kay and colleagues in the Learning Research Group at Xerox Palo Alto Research Center [PARC] propose the

Dynabook as a book-sized computer to run dynamic simulations for learning. Their *interim Dynabooks* are the first networked workstations.

1990s

Universities in Europe and Asia develop and evaluate mobile learning for students. Palm corporation offers grants to universities and companies who create and test the use of Mobile Learning on the PalmOS platform. Knowledgility creates the first mobile learning modules for CCNA, A+ and MCSE certification using the core tools that later became **LMA.**

2000s

The European Commission funds the major multi-national MOBIlearn and M-Learning projects.

Companies were formed that specialize in three core areas of mobile learning.

1. Authoring and publishing
2. Delivery and Tracking
3. Content Development

Conferences and trade shows were created to specifically deal with mobile learning and handheld education, including: mLearn, WMUTE, and IADIS Mobile Learning international conference series, ICML in Jordan, Mobile Learning in Malaysia, Handheld Learning in London, SALT Mobile in USA.

Analysis (Costs / Benefits, Forcast)

Value

The value of mobile learning —Tutors commented on the value of mobile learning as follows:

- It is important to bring new technology into the classroom.

- It will be more light weight device compare to books, PCs, etc.
- Mobile learning could be utilised as part of a learning approach which uses different types of activities (or a blended learning approach).
- Mobile learning supports the learning process rather than being integral to it.
- Mobile learning needs to be used appropriately, according to the groups of students involved.
- Mobile learning can be a useful add-on tool for students with special needs. However, for SMS and MMS this might be dependent on the students' specific disabilities or difficulties involved.
- Good IT support is needed.
- Mobile learning can be used as a 'hook' to re-engage disaffected youth.
- It is necessary to have enough devices for classroom use.

Challenges

Technical challenges include:

- Connectivity and battery life.
- Screen size and key size.
- Ability for authors to visualize mobile phones for delivery.
- Possibilities to meet required bandwidth for nonstop/ fast streaming.
- Number of file/asset's formats supported by a specific device.
- Content security or copyright issue from authoring group.
- Multiple standards, multiple screen sizes, multiple operating systems.

- Repurposing existing e-Learning materials for mobile platforms.

Social and educational challenges include:

- Accessibility and cost barriers for end users: Digital divide.
- How to assess learning outside the classroom?
- How to support learning across many contexts ?
- Content's security (or) pirating issues.
- Frequent changes in device models/technologies/ functionality etc.
- Developing an appropriate theory of learning for the mobile age.
- Conceptual differences between e- and m-learning.
- Design of technology to support a lifetime of learning.
- Tracking of results and proper use of this information.
- No restriction on learning timetable.
- Personal and private information and content.
- No demographic boundary.
- Disruption of students' personal and academic lives.
- Access to and use of the technology in developing countries.

Growth

Over the past ten years mobile learning has grown from a minor research interest to a set of significant projects in schools, workplaces, museums, cities and rural areas around the world. The mLearning community is still fragmented, with different national perspectives, differences between academia and industry, and between the school, higher education and lifelong learning sectors.

Current areas of growth include:

- Testing, surveys, job aids and just in time learning.
- Location-based and contextual learning.
- Social-networked mobile learning.
- Mobile educational gaming.
- "Lowest common denominator" mLearning to cellular phones using two way SMS messaging and voice-based CellCasting (podcasting to phones with interactive assessments).

According to a report by Ambient Insight in 2008, "the US market for Mobile Learning products and services is growing at a five-year compound annual growth rate (CAGR) of 21.7% and revenues reached $538 million in 2007. The data indicate that the demand is relatively immune from the recession." The findings of the report indicate that the largest demand throughout the forecast period is for custom development services, content conversion, and media services and that the healthcare sector accounts for 20% of the total US market for mobile learning.

Future

Technologies currently being researched for mobile learning include:

- Location aware learning.
- Point-and-shoot learning with camera phones and 2D codes.
- Near Field Communications (NFC) secure transactions.
- Sensors and accelerometers in mobile devices in behavioral based learning.
- Mobile content creation (including user generated content).
- Games and simulation for learning on mobile devices

- Context-aware ubiquitous learning.
- Augmented reality on mobile devices.

Delivery

While many think of mobile learning as delivering eLearning on small form factor devices, or often referred to as eLearning "lite", it has the potential to do much more than deliver courses, or parts of courses. It includes the use of mobile/handheld devices to perform any of the following:

- Deliver Education/Learning.
- Foster Communications/Collaboration.
- Conduct Assessments/Evaluations.
- Provide Access to Performance Support/Knowledge.

Today, any number of portable devices can quickly and easily deliver and support these functions. Cell or smartphones, multi-game devices, personal media players (PMPs), personal digital assistants (PDAs), or wireless single-purpose devices can help deliver coaching and mentoring, conduct assessments and evaluations (e.g., quizzes; tests; surveys/polls; and certifications), provide on-the-job support and access to information, education and references, and deliver podcasts, update alerts, forms and checklists. In these ways, mobile learning can enhance and support more traditional learning modes, making it more portable and accessible. Mobile devices can also serve as powerful data collection tools and facilitate the capture of user created content.

Approaches

In the Classroom

- Children and students using handheld computers, PDAs or handheld voting systems (such as clickers) in a classroom or lecture room.

- Students using mobile devices in the classroom to enhance group collaboration among students and instructors using a Pocket PC.

For Blended Learning

Mobile learning can provide support in order to enhance training that has been provided in a corporate business or other classroom environment.

Class Management

The mobile phone (through text SMS notices) can be used especially for distance education or students whose course requires them to be highly mobile and in particular to communicate information regarding availability of assignment results, venue changes and cancellations, etc.

Podcasting

Podcasting consists in listening to audio recordings of lectures, and can be used for instance to reinforce lecture and in particular to give the possibility for the student to rehearsal. It may be considered to have some influence on the traditional lectures.

Psychological research suggests that university students who download a podcast lecture achieve substantially higher exam results than those who attend the lecture in person, but only in the case when students take notes.

Podcasts maybe be delivered using syndication, although it should be noted that this method of delivery is not always easily adopted.

Outdoor

- Learning in museums or galleries with handheld or wearable technologies
- Learning outdoors, for example on field trips.

- Continuous learning and portable tools for military personnel.

At Work

- On the job training for someone who accesses training on a mobile device "just in time" to solve a problem or gain an update.

Life Long Learning and Self-Learning

The use of personal technology to support informal or lifelong learning, such as using handheld dictionaries and other devices for language learning.

Mobile technologies and approaches, i.e. Mobile Assisted Language Learning (MALL), are also used to assist in language learning. For instance handheld computers, cell phones, but also podcasting have been used for helping people to acquire a language.

Other

- Improving levels of literacy, numeracy and participation in education amongst young adults.
- Using the communication features of a mobile phone as part of a larger learning activity (e.g., sending media or texts into a central portfolio, or exporting audio files from a learning platform to your phone)

Technologies

Mobile devices and personal technologies that can support mobile learning, include:

- Personal Digital Assistant, in the classroom and outdoors
- UMPC, mobile phone, camera phone and Smart Phone
- Tablet PC
- Personal audio player, e.g. for listening to audio recordings of lectures (podcasting)

- Handheld audio and multimedia guides, in museums and galleries
- E-book
- Handheld game console, modern gaming consoles such as Sony PSP or Nintendo DS

Technical and delivery support for mobile learning:

- 3GP For compression and delivery method of audiovisual content associated with Mobile Learning
- Wi-Fi gives access to instructors and resources via internet
- GPRS mobile data service, provides high speed connection and data transfer rate

Authoring:

- Learning Mobile Author, e.g. for authoring and publishing WAP, Java ME and SmartPhone.

Relevant Organizations

- The International Association for Mobile Learning
    - o The International Association for Mobile Learning (IamLearn) has been formed as a membership organization to promote excellence in research, development and application of mobile and contextual learning. It organizes the annual mLearn international conference series. IamLearn manages a website to collate and disseminate information about new projects, emerging technologies, and teaching resources.

MNEMONIC

A **mnemonic** device is a mind memory and/or learning aid. Commonly, mnemonics are verbal—such as a very short poem or a special word used to help a person remember something—but may be visual, kinesthetic or auditory.

Mnemonics rely on associations between easy-to-remember constructs which can be related back to the data that is to be remembered. This is based on the principle that the human mind much more easily remembers spatial, personal, surprising, sexual or humorous or otherwise meaningful information than arbitrary sequences.

The word *mnemonic* is derived from the Ancient *mnemonikos* ("of memory") and is related to Mnemosyne ("remembrance"), the name of the goddess of memory in Greek mythology. Both of these words refer back to *mnema* ("remembrance"). Mnemonics in antiquity were most often considered in the context of what is today known as the Art of Memory.

The major assumption in antiquity was that there are two sorts of memory: the "natural" memory and the "artificial" memory. The former is inborn, and is the one that everyone uses every day. The artificial memory is one that is trained through learning and practicing a variety of mnemonic techniques. The latter can be used to perform feats of memory that are quite extraordinary, impossible to carry out using the natural memory alone.

First Letter Mnemonics

One common mnemonic for remembering lists consists of an easily remembered acronym, or phrase with an acronym that is associated with the list items. The idea lends itself well to memorizing hard-to-break passwords as well.

For example, to remember the "classic" named colours of the rainbow (Red, Orange, Yellow, Green, Blue, Indigo, Violet), it can be easier for some people to remember the mnemonics "Roy G. Biv" (a made-up name) instead. Or in reverse "VIBGYOR" pronouced "vib-GYOr".

Another example is an acrostic such as the Zoology mnemonic, used to remember the scientific classification applied in zoology.

Other Mnemonic Systems

- Art of Memory
- Method of loci
- Link System
- Mnemonic peg system
- Major system
- Mnemonic verses
- Goroawase System
- Dominic system

Arbitrariness of Mnemonics

A curious characteristic of many memory systems is that mnemonics work despite being (or possibly because of being) illogical or arbitrary. "Roy" is a legitimate first name, but there is no actual surname "Biv" and of course the middle initial "G" is arbitrary. Why is "Roy G. Biv" easy to remember in order to memorise the order that the seven colours of the rainbow appear? ROYGBIV can also be expressed as the almost meaningless phrase "Roy Great Britain the Fourth" again referencing "Roy" but using the GB national code for Great Britain and the Roman numerals for 4, viz: IV. The sentence "Richard of York gave battle in vain" is commonly used in the UK. The mnemonic for screw threads, "lefty loosey, righty tighty" only applies to half the circular arc when unscrewing or screwing in a nut, bolt or screw. It is reversed for the other half of the arc whereby any rightwards motion produces a torque which loosens the screw rather than tightens. Any two of the three months ending in -ember would fit just as euphoniously as September and November in "Thirty days hath...", yet most people can remember the rhyme correctly for a lifetime after having heard it once, and are never troubled by doubts as to *which* two of the -ember months have thirty days. A bizarre arbitrary association may stick in the mind better than a logical one.

One reason for the effectiveness of seemingly arbitrary mnemonics is the grouping of information provided by the mnemonic. Just as US phone numbers group 10 digits into three groups, the name "Roy G. Biv" groups seven colors into two short names and an initial. Various studies (most notably The Magical Number Seven, Plus or Minus Two) have shown that the human brain is capable of remembering only a limited number of arbitrary items in working memory; grouping these items into chunks permits the brain to hold more of them in memory.

Assembly Mnemonics

In assembly language a mnemonic is a code, usually from 1 to 5 letters, that represents an opcode, followed by one or more numbers (the operands).

Programming in machine code, by supplying the computer with the numbers of the operations it must perform, can be quite a burden, because for every operation the corresponding number must be looked up or remembered. Looking up all numbers takes a lot of time, and mis-remembering a number may introduce computer bugs.

Therefore a set of mnemonics was devised. Each number was represented by an alphabetic code. So instead of entering the number corresponding to addition to add two numbers one can enter "add". Although mnemonics differ between different CPU designs some are common, for instance: "sub" (subtract), "div" (divide), "add" (add) and "mul" (multiply).

This type of mnemonic is different from the ones listed above in that instead of a way to make remembering numbers easier, it is a way to make remembering numbers unnecessary (e.g. by relying on the computer's assembler program to do the lookup work).

Assembler mnemonics do not necessarily have a one-to-one correspondence with opcodes. Sometimes, the same mnemonic is used for distinct (but related) operations, such as using "add" for both register+register and register+constant. Conversely, multiple mnemonics may use the same opcode: For example, if a processor has a "branch if less than" instruction but no "branch if greater than" instruction, a separate instruction mnemonic may be defined for "branch if greater than" and implemented as a "branch if less than" instruction with the operands reversed.

Mnemonics in Foreign Language Acquisition

Mnemonics can be helpful in studying a foreign language, for example by adapting a foreign word that is hard to remember to a pre-existent phrase in the learner's native language - using folk etymology. This technique is also known as the "keyword mnemonic". Linguist Ghil'ad Zuckermann has proposed many Anglo-Hebraic lexical mnemonics for English-speaking students of Israeli Hebrew. For example, in trying to assist the learner to remember **ohel**, the Hebrew word for *tent*, Zuckermann proposes the memorable sentence "**Oh hell**, there's a raccoon in my *tent*". The memorable sentence "There's a *fork* in **Ma's leg**" may help the learner remember that the Hebrew word for *fork* is **mazleg**, and so forth. The notable linguist Michel Thomas taught students to remember that *estar* is a Spanish verb for *to be* by using the phrase "to be a star". The acronym mnemonic "bangs" is used to help students of French to remember which adjectives go before the noun, "Beauty, Age, Number, Goodness, and Size". Also, phrases of position in French can easily be remembered with sentences, e.g. for 'pres de', meaning 'near to': "when you PRAY, you are NEAR TO God"; 'loin de', far from: "RWANDA is FAR FROM here", and 'a cote de', next to: "COATs on a hook are NEXT TO each other".

●●

6
Multimedia Learning

Multimedia learning is the common name used to describe the cognitive theory of multimedia learning This theory encompasses several principles of learning with multimedia.

The Modality Principle

When learning with multimedia the brain must simultaneously encode two different types of information, an auditory stimulus and a visual stimulus. One might expect that these competing sources of information would tend to overwhelm or overload the learner. However, psychological research has shown that verbal information is in fact better remembered when accompanied by a visual image. Baddeley and Hitch proposed a theory of working memory which has two largely independent subcomponents that tend to work in parallel - one visual and one verbal/acoustic. This allows us to simultaneously process information coming from our eyes and ears. Thus a learner is not necessarily overwhelmed or overloaded by multimodal instruction, and it can in fact be beneficial.

The finding that items presented both visually and verbally are better remembered gave rise to dual-coding theory, first proposed by Paivio and later applied to multimedia by Richard Mayer and his associates. Mayer has shown learners are better able to transfer their learning given multimodal instruction. Mayer explains the modality effect from an information processing/cognitive load perspective.

In a series of studies Mayer and his colleagues tested Paivio's dual-coding theory, with multimedia. They repeatedly found that students learning given multimedia with animation and narration consistently did better on transfer questions than those who learn from animation and text-based materials. That is, they were significantly better when it came to applying what they had learned after receiving multimedia rather than mono-media (visual only) instruction. These results were then later confirmed by other groups of researchers.

Initially the instructional content of these multimedia learning studies was limited to logical scientific processes that centered on cause-and-effect systems like automobile braking systems, how a bicycle pump works, or cloud formation. But eventually it was found that the modality effect could be extended to other domains, which were not necessarily cause-and-effect based systems.

Information then can and should be encoded as both as visually and auditory (narration). If verbal information is encoded auditorily it reduces the cognitive load of the learner and they are better able to handle that incoming information. Mayer has since called this the "Modality effect," or the Modality Principle. This was one of the many principles of his "Cognitive Theory of Multimedia Learning".

The Redundancy Principle

According to this principle: "Students learn better from animation and narration than from animation, narration, and on-screen text."

Thus it's better to eliminate redundant material. This is because learners do not learn as well, when they both hear and see the same verbal message during a presentation. This is a special case of the Split attention effect of Sweller and Chandler.

Other Principles

- **Spatial Contiguity Principle** — "Students learn better when corresponding words and pictures are presented near rather than far from each other on the page or screen."
- **Temporal Contiguity Principle**—"Students learn better when corresponding words and pictures are presented simultaneously rather than successively."
- **Coherence Principle** — "Students learn better when extraneous material is excluded rather than included."
- **Individual Differences Principle** — "Design effects are stronger for low-knowledge learners than for high knowledge learners, and for high-spatial learners rather than for low-spatial learners."

Challenges to the Application of Principles

Not all research has found that the principles of multimedia learning apply generally outside of laboratory conditions. For example, Muller, Lee, and Sharma found that the coherence principle did not transfer to an authentic learning environment. In their study, adding approximately 50% additional extraneous but interesting material did not result in any significant difference in learner performance. These authors suggest that additional interesting information may help maintain the learner's interest in authentic learning environments.

OFFICE OF DISTANCE EDUCATION

The **Office of Distance Education (ODE)** was founded in July 1998 on the campus of the Arkansas School for Mathematics, Sciences and the Arts in Hot Springs, Arkansas.

Conceived as a way to expand educational opportunities in Arkansas' rural schools, the Office of Distance Education uses H.323-based video conferencing and asynchronous technologies to provide highly qualified, fully certified teachers to school districts unable to hire qualified faculty locally.

During its first year of operation, ODE enrolled 228 high school students from 23 school districts. More than 2,300 students from approximately eighty districts currently receive instruction from ODE.

ODE offers complete elementary, middle grades and high school curricula as well as College Board-approved Advanced Placement courses and Concurrent Enrollment courses that allow students to earn college credit. A founding member of the Mid-South Distance Education Partnership, ODE classes are now available to school districts throughout the United States. ODE's programmes are accredited by the North Central Association Commission on Accreditation and School Improvement.

Online Degrees

The term **online degrees** refers to college degrees (sometimes including high school diplomas and non-degree certificate programs) that can be earned primarily or entirely through the use of an Internet-connected computer, rather than attending college in a traditional campus setting. Improvements in technology and the increasing use of the Internet worldwide have led to a proliferation of online colleges that award associate's, bachelor's, master's and doctoral degrees.

Accreditation

The goal of educational accreditation, is to ensure that programmes provided by institutions of higher education meet acceptable levels of quality. In the area of online education, it is important to avoid diploma mills that offer fake degrees at a cost. Students seeking valid online degrees should **obtain proof of accreditation** from a regional or national/specialized accrediting body in the United States. Online colleges that are fully accredited have earned a widely recognized form of university accreditation from one of six regional accreditation boards.

There are **six regional accreditation boards**:

- Middle States Association of Colleges and Schools.
- Northwest Commission on Colleges and Universities.
- North Central Association of Colleges and Schools.
- New England Association of Schools and Colleges.
- Southern Association of Colleges and Schools.
- Western Association of Schools and Colleges.

Quality of Learning Online

Online education is a proven model for learning, with a lengthy track record. It enables accredited higher learning for individuals living with physical disabilities, busy working class people, soldiers and those living abroad, and stay at home parents to mention a few. There is fundamentally little difference between physically sitting in an auditorium listening to lectures versus watching a webcasted video of the professor.

The recognition of the quality of online degrees compared to on-campus degrees varies. While most major online colleges are regionally accredited, the public perception of their quality is in dispute. Some experts argue that degrees in certain fields are more accepted online than in others, while some programs are less suited for online-only schools.

A survey by the Distance Education and Training Council found that 100 percent of employers who responded felt that distance education programme graduates performed better on the job as a result of their degree (as compared to their previous performance). Additionally, employers felt that an employee receiving a distance education degree compared favourably, in terms of knowledge learned, to someone with a resident degree.

In some instances, an online degree may be no different than a degree earned in a campus-based program. The instruction is often exactly the same, and the online degree contains no special designation. An example of this is the degree offered to Columbia University students who earn a degree through the Columbia Video Network (CVN) versus the campus-based programme.

Prevalence of Online Education

In USA the National Center for Education Statistics (NCES) conducted a distance education study based on the 2001-2002 academic year at 2-year and 4-year Title IV (Federal Student Aid)-eligible, degree-granting institutions. The study reported that 56 percent of all institutions surveyed offered distance education courses. The study also found that public institutions were more likely to offer distance education than were private institutions.

Operant Conditioning

Operant conditioning is the use of consequences to modify the occurrence and form of behaviour. Operant conditioning is distinguished from classical conditioning (also called respondent conditioning, or Pavlovian conditioning) in that operant conditioning deals with the modification of "voluntary behaviour" or operant behaviour. Operant behaviour "operates" on the environment and is maintained by its consequences, while classical conditioning deals with the conditioning of respondent behaviours which are elicited by antecedent conditions. Behaviours conditioned via a classical conditioning procedure are not maintained by consequences. The main dependent variable is the rate of response that is developed over a period of time. New operant responses can be further developed and shaped by reinforcing close approximations of the desired response.

It's important to note that organisms are not spoken of as being reinforced, punished, or extinguished; it is the response that is reinforced, punished, or extinguished. Additionally, reinforcement, punishment, and extinction are not terms whose use is restricted to the laboratory. Naturally occurring consequences can also be said to reinforce, punish, or extinguish behaviour and are not always delivered by people.

- **Reinforcement** is a consequence that causes a behaviour to occur with greater frequency.
- **Punishment** is a consequence that causes a behaviour to occur with less frequency.
- **Extinction** is the lack of any consequence following a behaviour. When a behaviour is inconsequential, producing neither favorable nor unfavourable consequences, it will occur with less frequency. When a previously reinforced behaviour is no longer reinforced with either positive or negative reinforcement, it leads to a decline in the response.

Four contexts of operant conditioning: Here the terms *"positive"* and *"negative"* are not used in their popular sense, but rather: *"positive"* refers to addition, and *"negative"* refers to subtraction.

What is added or subtracted may be either reinforcement or punishment. Hence ***positive** punishment* is sometimes a confusing term, as it denotes the **addition** of a stimulus or increase in the intensity of a stimulus that is aversive (such as spanking or an electric shock) The four procedures are:

1. **Positive reinforcement**(Reinforcement) occurs when a behaviour (response) is followed by a favourable

stimulus (commonly seen as pleasant) that increases the frequency of that behaviour.

2. **Negative reinforcement**(Escape) occurs when a behaviour (response) is followed by the removal of an aversive stimulus (commonly seen as unpleasant) thereby increasing that behaviour's frequency.
3. **Positive punishment**(Punishment) (also called "Punishment by contingent stimulation") occurs when a behaviour (response) is followed by an aversive stimulus, such as introducing a shock or loud noise, resulting in a decrease in that behaviour.
4. **Negative punishment**(Penalty) (also called "Punishment by contingent withdrawal") occurs when a behaviour (response) is followed by the removal of a favourable stimulus, such as taking away a child's toy following an undesired behaviour, resulting in a decrease in that behaviour.

Also:

- **Avoidance learning** is a type of learning in which a certain behaviour results in the cessation of an aversive stimulus. For example, performing the behaviour of shielding one's eyes when in the sunlight (or going indoors) will help avoid the aversive stimulation of having light in one's eyes.
- **Extinction** occurs when a behaviour (response) that had previously been reinforced is no longer effective.
- **Noncontingent reinforcement** refers to delivery of reinforcing stimuli regardless of the organism's (aberrant) behaviour. The idea is that the target behaviour decreases because it is no longer necessary to receive the reinforcement. This typically entails time-based delivery of stimuli identified as maintaining aberrant behavior, which serves to decrease the rate of

the target behaviour. As no measured behaviour is identified as being strengthened, there is controversy surrounding the use of the term noncontingent "reinforcement".

Thorndike's Law of Effect

Operant conditioning, sometimes called *instrumental conditioning* or *instrumental learning*, was first extensively studied by Edward L. Thorndike (1874-1949), who observed the behaviour of cats trying to escape from home-made puzzle boxes. When first constrained in the boxes, the cats took a long time to escape. With experience, ineffective responses occurred less frequently and successful responses occurred more frequently, enabling the cats to escape in less time over successive trials. In his Law of Effect, Thorndike theorized that successful responses, those producing *satisfying* consequences, were "stamped in" by the experience and thus occurred more frequently. Unsuccessful responses, those producing *annoying* consequences, were *stamped out* and subsequently occurred less frequently. In short, some consequences *strengthened* behavior and some consequences *weakened* behaviour. Thorndike produced the first known learning curves through this procedure. B.F. Skinner (1904-1990) formulated a more detailed analysis of operant conditioning based on reinforcement, punishment, and extinction. Following the ideas of Ernst Mach, Skinner rejected Thorndike's mediating structures required by "satisfaction" and constructed a new conceptualization of behaviour without any such references. So while experimenting with some homemade feeding mechanisms Skinner invented the operant conditioning chamber which allowed him to measure rate of response as a key dependent variable using a cumulative record of lever presses or key pecks.

Operant Conditioning *vs* Fixed Action Patterns

Skinner's construct of instrumental learning is contrasted with what Nobel Prize winning biologist Konrad Lorenz termed "fixed action patterns," or reflexive, impulsive, or instinctive behaviours. These behaviours were said by Skinner and others to exist outside the parameters of operant conditioning but were considered essential to a comprehensive analysis of behaviour.

Fixed Action Patterns have their origin in the genetic makeup of the animal in question. Examples of "fixed action patterns" include ducklings that will follow any moving object if they see that object within the period of time when the behaviour will be released, or the dance that a bee performs. Characteristics of "fixed action patterns" include not needing to be learned or acquired; these behaviours are performed correctly the first time that they are performed.

Within operant conditioning, Fixed Action Patterns can be used as reinforcers for learned behaviours. Often, fixed action patterns such as predatory grabbing in dogs can be used as a reinforcer. In police and military dog training, the desire to engage in the predatory bite is often used as a reinforcement for successful completion of a search or an obedience exercise. The amount of desire that a dog might have to engage in the fixed action pattern is also known as "prey drive" although this may well be a misnomer as there is no quantification for how much a dog wants to engage in the predatory sequence.

Fixed Action Patterns can also get in the way of successful learning. Breland and Breland note in their paper "The Mis-Behaviour of Organisms" that raccoons cannot be taught to place an item in a jar due to the fixed action pattern that is released when they begin to place the item in the jar. When a component of a learned sequence triggers the beginning of a fixed action pattern, it is difficult and sometimes impossible to interrupt that sequence before it is completed. In this way, teaching raccoons to place items in jars, pigs to fetch (fetching triggers routing behaviours) or young ducklings to sit and stay.

Criticisms

Thorndike's law of effect specifically requires that a behaviour be followed by satisfying consequences for learning to occur. There are, however, cases in which learning can be shown to occur without good or bad effects following the behaviour. For instance, a number of experiments examining the phenomenon of latent learning showed that a rat needn't receive a satisfying reward (food, if hungry; water, if thirsty) in order to learn a maze; learning that becomes apparent immediately after the desired reward is introduced. However, views claiming such research invalidates theories of operant conditioning are molecular to a fault. If the rat has a history of "searching behaviour" being reinforced in novel environments, the behaviour will occur in new environments. This is especially plausible in a species which scavenges for food and has thus likely inherited a propensity for searching behaviour to be sensitive to reinforcement. Behaving during initial extinction trials as the organism had during reinforcement trials is not proof of latent learning, as behaviour is a function of the history of the individual organism and its genetic endowment and is never controlled by future consequences. That an organism continues to respond during unreinforced trials has been well-established when studying intermittent schedules of reinforcement.

A different experiment, in humans, showed that "punishing" the correct behaviour may actually cause it to be more frequently taken (i.e. stamp it in). Subjects are given a number of pairs of holes on a large board and required to learn which hole to poke a stylus through for each pair. If the subjects receive an electric shock for punching the correct hole, they learn which hole is correct more quickly than subjects who receive an electric shock for punching the incorrect hole. This cannot, however, be accurately described as punishment if it is increasing the probability of the behaviour.

Biological Correlates of Operant Conditioning

The first scientific studies identifying neurons that responded in ways that suggested they encode for conditioned stimuli came from work by Rusty Richardson and Mahlon deLong. They showed that nucleus basalis neurons, which release acetylcholine broadly throughout the cerebral cortex, are activated shortly after a conditioned stimulus, or after a primary reward if no conditioned stimulus exists. These neurons are equally active for positive and negative reinforcers, and have been demonstrated to cause plasticity in many cortical regions. Evidence also exists that dopamine is activated at similar times. There is considerable evidence that dopamine participate in both reinforcement and aversive learning. Dopamine pathways project much more densely onto frontal cortex regions. Cholinergic projections, in contrast, are dense even in the posterior cortical regions like the primary visual cortex. A study of patients with Parkinson's disease, a condition attributed to the insufficient action of dopamine, further illustrates the role of dopamine in positive reinforcement. It showed that while off their medication, patients learned more readily with aversive consequences than with positive reinforcement. Patients who were on their medication showed the opposite to be the case, positive reinforcement proving to be the more effective form of learning when the action of dopamine is high.

Factors that Alter the Effectiveness of Consequences

When using consequences to modify a response, the effectiveness of a consequence can be increased or decreased by various factors. These factors can apply to either reinforcing or punishing consequences.

1. **Satiation/Deprivation:** The effectiveness of a consequence will be reduced if the individual's "appetite" for that source of stimulation has been

satisfied. Inversely, the effectiveness of a consequence will increase as the individual becomes deprived of that stimulus. If someone is not hungry, food will not be an effective reinforcer for behaviour. Satiation is generally only a potential problem with primary reinforcers, those that do not need to be learned such as food and water.

2. **Immediacy:** After a response, how immediately a consequence is then felt determines the effectiveness of the consequence. More immediate feedback will be more effective than less immediate feedback. If someone's license plate is caught by a traffic camera for speeding and they receive a speeding ticket in the mail a week later, this consequence will not be very effective against speeding. But if someone is speeding and is caught in the act by an officer who pulls them over, then their speeding behavior is more likely to be affected.

3. **Contingency:** If a consequence does not contingently (reliably, or consistently) follow the target response, its effectiveness upon the response is reduced. But if a consequence follows the response consistently after successive instances, its ability to modify the response is increased. The schedule of reinforcement, when consistent, leads to faster learning. When the schedule is variable the learning is slower. Extinction is more difficult when learning occurred during intermittent reinforcement and more easily extinguished when learning occurred during a highly consistent schedule.

4. **Size:** This is a "cost-benefit" determinant of whether a consequence will be effective. If the size, or amount, of the consequence is large enough to be worth the effort, the consequence will be more effective upon the behaviour. An unusually large lottery jackpot, for example, might be enough to get someone to buy a

one-dollar lottery ticket (or even buying multiple tickets). But if a lottery jackpot is small, the same person might not feel it to be worth the effort of driving out and finding a place to buy a ticket. In this example, it's also useful to note that "effort" is a punishing consequence. How these opposing expected consequences (reinforcing and punishing) balance out will determine whether the behaviour is performed or not.

Most of these factors exist for biological reasons. The biological purpose of the Principle of Satiation is to maintain the organism's homeostasis. When an organism has been deprived of sugar, for example, the effectiveness of the taste of sugar as a reinforcer is high. However, as the organism reaches or exceeds their optimum blood-sugar levels, the taste of sugar becomes less effective, perhaps even aversive.

The principles of Immediacy and Contingency exist for neurochemical reasons. When an organism experiences a reinforcing stimulus, dopamine pathways in the brain are activated. This network of pathways "releases a short pulse of dopamine onto many dendrites, thus broadcasting a rather global reinforcement signal to postsynaptic neurons." This results in the plasticity of these synapses allowing recently activated synapses to increase their sensitivity to efferent signals, hence increasing the probability of occurrence for the recent responses preceding the reinforcement. These responses are, statistically, the most likely to have been the behaviour responsible for successfully achieving reinforcement. But when the application of reinforcement is either less immediate or less contingent (less consistent), the ability of dopamine to act upon the appropriate synapses is reduced.

Operant Variability

Operant variability is what allows a response to adapt to new situations. Operant behaviour is distinguished from reflexes in that its **response topography** (the form of the response) is subject to slight variations from one performance to another. These slight variations can include small differences in the specific motions involved, differences in the amount of force applied, and small changes in the timing of the response. If a subject's history of reinforcement is consistent, such variations will remain stable because the same successful variations are more likely to be reinforced than less successful variations. However, behavioural variability can also be altered when subjected to certain controlling variables.

An **extinction burst** will often occur when an extinction procedure has just begun. This consists of a sudden and temporary *increase* in the response's frequency, followed by the eventual decline and extinction of the behaviour targeted for elimination. Take, as an example, a pigeon that has been reinforced to peck an electronic button. During its training history, every time the pigeon pecked the button, it will have received a small amount of bird seed as a reinforcer. So, whenever the bird is hungry, it will peck the button to receive food. However, if the button were to be turned off, the hungry pigeon will first try pecking the button just as it has in the past. When no food is forthcoming, the bird will likely try again... and again, and again. After a period of frantic activity, in which their pecking behaviour yields no result, the pigeon's pecking will decrease in frequency.

The evolutionary advantage of this **extinction burst** is clear. In a natural environment, an animal that persists in a learned behaviour, despite not resulting in immediate reinforcement, might still have a chance of producing reinforcing consequences if they try again. This animal would be at an advantage over another animal that gives up too easily.

Extinction-induced variability serves a similar adaptive role. When extinction begins, and if the environment allows for it, an initial increase in the response rate is not the only thing that can happen. Imagine a bell curve. The horizontal axis would represent the different variations possible for a given behaviour. The vertical axis would represent the response's probability in a given situation. Response variants in the middle of the bell curve, at its highest point, are the most likely because those responses, according to the organism's experience, have been the most effective at producing reinforcement. The more extreme forms of the behaviour would lie at the lower ends of the curve, to the left and to the right of the peak, where their probability for expression is low.

A simple example would be a person inside a room opening a door to exit. The response would be the opening of the door, and the reinforcer would be the freedom to exit. For each time that same person opens that same door, they do not open the door in the exact same way every time. Rather, each time they open the door a little differently: sometimes with less force, sometimes with more force; sometimes with one hand, sometimes with the other hand; sometimes more quickly, sometimes more slowly. Because of the physical properties of the door and its handle, there is a certain range of successful responses which are reinforced.

Now imagine in our example that the subject tries to open the door and it won't budge. This is when **extinction-induced variability** occurs. The bell curve of probable responses will begin to broaden, with more extreme forms of behaviour becoming more likely. The person might now try opening the door with extra force, repeatedly twist the knob, try to hit the door with their shoulder, may be even call for help or climb out a window. This is how extinction causes variability in behaviour, in the hope that these new variations might be successful. For this reason, **extinction-induced variability** is an important part of the operant procedure of **shaping**.

Avoidance Learning

Avoidance training belongs to negative reinforcement schedules. The subject learns that a certain response will result in the termination or prevention of an aversive stimulus. There are two kinds of commonly used experimental settings: discriminated and free-operant avoidance learning.

Discriminated avoidance learning

In discriminated avoidance learning, a novel stimulus such as a light or a tone is followed by an aversive stimulus such as a shock (CS-US, similar to classical conditioning). During the first trials (called escape-trials) the animal usually experiences both the CS (Conditioned Stimulus) and the US (Unconditioned Stimulus), showing the operant response to terminate the aversive US. By the time, the animal will learn to perform the response already during the presentation of the CS thus preventing the aversive US from occurring. Such trials are called avoidance trials.

Free-operant avoidance learning

In this experimental session, no discrete stimulus is used to signal the occurrence of the aversive stimulus. Rather, the aversive stimulus (mostly shocks) are presented without explicit warning stimuli.

There are two crucial time intervals determining the rate of avoidance learning. This first one is called the S-S-interval (shock-shock-interval). This is the amount of time which passes during successive presentations of the shock (unless the operant response is performed). The other one is called the R-S-interval (response-shock-interval) which specifies the length of the time interval following an operant response during which no shocks will be delivered. Note that each time the organism performs the operant response, the R-S-interval without shocks begins anew.

Two-Process Theory of Avoidance

This theory was originally established to explain learning in discriminated avoidance learning. It assumes two processes to take place. *(a) Classical conditioning of fear.* During the first trials of the training, the organism experiences both CS and aversive US (escape-trials). The theory assumed that during those trials classical conditioning takes place by pairing the CS with the US. Because of the aversive nature of the US the CS is supposed to elicit a conditioned emotional reaction (CER) — fear. In classical conditioning, presenting a CS conditioned with an aversive US disrupts the organism's ongoing behaviour. *(b) Reinforcement of the operant response by fear-reduction.* Because during the first process, the CS signalling the aversive US has itself become aversive by eliciting fear in the organism, reducing this unpleasant emotional reaction serves to motivate the operant response. The organism learns to make the response during the US, thus terminating the aversive internal reaction elicited by the CS. An important aspect of this theory is that the term "Avoidance" does not really describe what the organism is doing. It does not "avoid" the aversive US in the sense of anticipating it. Rather the organism escapes an aversive internal state, caused by the CS.

- One of the practical aspects of operant conditioning with relation to animal training is the use of shaping (reinforcing successive approximations and not reinforcing behavior past approximating), as well as chaining.

Verbal Behaviour

In 1957 Skinner published Verbal Behaviour a theoretical extension of the work he had pioneered since 1938. This work extended the theory of operant conditioning to human behaviour previously assigned to the areas of language, linguistics and other areas. Verbal Behaviour is the logical extension of Skinner's ideas, in which he introduced new functional relationship categories such as intraverbals, autoclitics, mands, tacts and the controlling relationship of the audience. All of these relationships were based on operant conditioning and relied on no new mechanisms despite the introduction of new functional categories.

Four Term Contingency

Applied behaviour analysis, which is the name of the discipline directly descended from Skinner's work, holds that behaviour is explained in four terms: conditional stimulus (S^C), a discriminative stimulus (S^d), a response (R), and a reinforcing stimulus (S^{rein} or S^r for reinforcers, sometimes S^{ave} for aversive stimuli).

Operant Hoarding

Operant Hoarding is a term referring to the choice made by a rat, on a compound schedule called a multiple schedule, that maximizes its rate of reinforcement in an operant conditioning context. More specifically, rats were shown to have allowed food pellets to accumulate in a food tray by continuing to press a lever on a continuous reinforcement schedule instead of retrieving those pellets. Retrieval of the pellets always instituted a one-minute period of extinction during which no additional food pellets were available but those that had been accumulated earlier could be consumed. This finding appears to contradict the usual finding that rats behave impulsively in situations in which there is a choice between a smaller food object right away and a larger food object after some delay. See schedules of reinforcement.

●●

7
Applied Behaviour Analysis

Applied behaviour analysis (ABA) is the science of applying experimentally derived principles of behaviour to improve socially significant behaviour. ABA takes what we know about behaviour and uses it to bring about positive change (Applied). Behaviours are defined in observable and measurable terms in order to assess change over time (Behaviour). The behaviour is analyzed within the environment to determine what factors are influencing the behaviour (Analysis). Applied behaviour analysis contributes to a full range of areas including: AIDS prevention, conservation of natural resources, education, gerontology, health and exercise, industrial safety, language acquisition, littering, medical procedures, parenting, seatbelt use, severe mental disorders, sports, and zoo management and care of animals. ABA-based interventions are used to treat people with a wide variety of behaviours and diagnoses, notably autism spectrum disorders.

ABA is defined as the science in which the principles of the analysis of behaviour are applied systematically to improve socially significant behaviour, and in which experimentation is used to identify the variables responsible for change in behaviour. It is one of the three fields of behaviour analysis. The other two are behaviourism, or the philosophy of the science; and experimental analysis of behaviour, or basic experimental research.

Baer, Wolf, and Risley's 1968 article is still used as the standard description of ABA. It describes the seven dimensions of ABA: application; a focus on behaviour; the use of analysis; and its technological, conceptually systematic, effective, and general approach.

Characteristics

Baer, Wolf, and Risley's seven dimensions are:

- **Applied**: ABA focuses on areas that are of social significance. In doing this, behaviour scientists must take into consideration more than just the short-term behaviour change, but also look at how behaviour changes can affect the consumer, those who are close to the consumer, and how any change will affect the interactions between the two.
- **Behavioral**: ABA must be behavioural, i.e.: behaviour itself must change, not just what the consumer SAYS about the behaviour. It is not the goal of the behaviour scientists to get their consumers to stop complaining about behaviour problems, but rather to change the problem behaviour itself. In addition, behaviour must be objectively measured. A behaviour scientist can not resort to the measurement of non-behavioural substitutes.
- **Analytic**: The behaviour scientist can demonstrate believable control over the behaviour that is being changed. In the lab, this has been easy as the researcher can start and stop the behaviour at will. However, in the applied situation, this is not always as easy, nor ethical, to do. According to Baer, Wolf, and Risley, this difficulty should not stop a science from upholding the strength of its principles. As such, they referred to two designs that are best used in applied settings to demonstrate control and maintain ethical standards. These are the reversal and multiple baseline designs. The reversal design is one in which the behaviour of

choice is measured prior to any intervention. Once the pattern appears stable, an intervention is introduced, and behaviour is measured. If there is a change in behaviour, measurement continues until the new pattern of behaviour appears stable. Then, the intervention is removed, or reduced, and the behaviour is measured to see if it changes again. If the behaviour scientist truly has demonstrated control of the behaviour with the intervention, the behaviour of interest should change with intervention changes.

- **Technological**: This means that if any other researcher were to read the study's description, that researcher would be able to "replicate the application with the same results". This means that the description must be very detailed and clear. Ambiguous descriptions do not qualify. Cooper *et al.* describe a good check for the technological characteristic: "have a person trained in applied behaviour analysis carefully read the description and then act out the procedure in detail. If the person makes any mistakes, adds any operations, omits any steps, or has to ask any questions to clarify the written description then the description is not sufficiently technological and requires improvement."

- **Conceptually Systematic**: A defining characteristic is in regards to the interventions utilized; and thus research must be conceptually systematic by only utilizing procedures and interpreting results of these procedures in terms of the principles from which they were derived.

- **Effective**: An application of these techniques improve behaviour under investigation. Specifically, it is not a theoretical importance of the variable, but rather the practical importance (social importance) that is essential.

- **Generality**: It should last over time, in different environments, and spread to other behaviours not directly treated by the intervention. In addition, continued change in specified behaviour after intervention for that behaviour has been withdrawn is also an example of generality.

In 2005, Heward, *et al.* added the following five characteristics:

- **Accountable**: Direct and frequent measurement enables analysts to detect their success and failures to make changes in an effort to increase successes while decreasing failures. ABA is a scientific approach in which analysts may guess but then critically test ideas, rather than "guess and guess again". This constant revision of techniques, commitment to effectiveness and analysis of results leads to an accountable science.

- **Public**: Applied behaviour analysis is completely visible and public. This means that there are no explanations that cannot be observed. There are no mystical, metaphysical explanations, hidden treatment, or magic. Thus, ABA is produces results whose explanations are available to all of the public.

- **Doable**: ABA has a pragmatic element in that implementors of interventions can consist of a variety of individuals, from teachers to the participants themselves. This does not mean that ABA requires one simply to learn a few procedures, but with the proper planning, it can effectively be implemented by most everyone willing to invest the effort.

- **Empowering**: ABA provides tools to practitioners that allow them to effectively change behaviour. By constantly providing visual feedback to the practitioner on the results of the intervention, this feature of ABA allows clinicians to assess their skill level and builds confidence in their technology.

- **Optimistic**: According to several leading authors, practitioners skilled in behaviour analysis have genuine cause to be optimistic for the following reasons:
- The environmental view is essentially optimistic as it suggests that all individuals possess roughly equal potential.
- Direct and continuous measurements enable practitioners to detect small improvements in performance that might have otherwise been missed.
- As a practitioner uses behavioural techniques with positive outcomes, the more they will become optimistic about future success prospects.
- The literature provides many examples of success teaching individuals considered previously unteachable.

Concepts

Behaviour

Behaviour is the activity of living organisms. Human behaviour is the entire gamut of what people do including thinking and feeling. Behaviour can be determined by applying the Dead Man's test:

> "If a dead man can do it, it ain't behaviour. And if a dead man can't do it, then it is behaviour"

Behaviour is that portion of an organism's interaction with its environment that is characterized by detectable displacement in space through time of some part of the organism and that results in a measurable change in at least one aspect of the environment. Often, the term behaviour is used to reference a larger class of responses that share physical dimensions or function. In this instance, the term *response* indicates a single instance of that behaviour. If a group of responses have the same function, this group can be classified as a response class. Finally, when discussing a person's collection of behaviour, repertoire is used. It can either pertain specifically to a set of response classes that are relevant to a particular situation, or it can refer to every behaviour that a person can do.

Operant Conditioning

Operant behaviour is that which is selected by its consequences. The conditioning of operant behaviour is the result of reinforcement and punishment. Operant conditioning applies to voluntary responses, which an organism performs deliberately, to produce a desirable outcome. The term operant emphasizes this point;the organism operates on its environment to produce some desirable result. For example, operant conditioning is at work when we learn that toiling industriously can bring about a raise or that studying hard results in good grade.

Respondent Conditioning

All organisms respond in predictable ways to certain stimuli. These stimulus-response relations are called reflexes. The response component of the reflex is called respondent behaviour. It is defined as behaviour which is elicited by antecedent stimuli. Respondent conditioning (also called Classical Conditioning) is learning in which new stimuli acquire the ability to elicit respondents. This is done through stimulus-stimulus pairing, for example, the stimulus (smell of food) can elicit a person's salivation. By pairing that stimulus (smell) with another stimulus (word "food"), the second stimulus can obtain the function

Environment

The environment is the entire constellation of circumstances in which an organism exists. This includes events both inside and outside of an organism, but only real physical events are included. The environment consists of stimuli. A stimulus is an "energy change that affects an organism through its receptor cells."

A stimulus can be described:

Formally by its physical features.

Temporally by when they occur in respect to the behaviour.

Functionally by their effect on behaviour.

Reinforcement

Reinforcement is the most important principle of behaviour and a key element of most behaviour change programmes. It is the process by which behaviour is strengthened, if a behaviour is followed closely in time by a stimulus and this results in an increase in the future frequency of that behaviour. The addition of a stimulus following an event that serves as a reinforcer is termed positive reinforcement. If the removal of an event serves as a reinforcer, this is termed negative reinforcement. There are multiple schedules of reinforcement that effect the future frequency of behaviour.

Punishment

Punishment is a process by which a consequence immediately follows a behaviour which decreases the future frequency of that behaviour. Like reinforcement, a stimulus can be added (positive punishment) or removed (negative punishment). Broadly, there are three types of punishment: presentation of aversive stimuli, response cost and time out. Punishment in practice can often result in unwanted side effects, and has as such been used only after reinforcement-only procedures have failed to work. Unwanted side effects can include the increase in other unwanted behaviour as well as a decrease in desired behaviours. Some other potential unwanted effects include escape and avoidance, emotional behaviour, and can result in behavioural contrast.

Extinction

Extinction is the technical term to describe the procedure of withholding/discontinuing reinforcement of a previously reinforced behaviour, resulting in the decrease of that behaviour. The behaviour is then set to be extinguished. Extinction procedures are often preferred over punishment procures that are frequently deemed unethical and in many states prohibited. Nonetheless, extinction procedures must be implemented with utmost care by professionals, as they are generally associated with extinction bursts. An extinction burst is the temporary increase in the frequency, intensity, and/or duration of the behaviour targeted for extinction. Other characteristics of an extinction burst include *(a)* extinction-produced aggression—the occurrence of an emotional response to an extinction procedure often manifested as aggression; and *(b)* extinction-induced response variability — the occurrence of novel behaviours that did not typically occur prior to the extinction procedure. These novel behaviours are a core component of shaping procedures.

Discriminated Operant and Three-term Contingency

In addition to a relation being made between behaviour and its consequences, operant conditioning also establishes relations between antecedent conditions and behaviours. This differs from the S-R formulations (If-A-then-B), and replaces it with an AB-because-of-C formulation. In other words, the relation between a behaviour(B) and its context(A) is because of consequences (C), more specifically, this relationship between AB because of C indicates that the relationship is established by prior consequences that have occurred in similar contexts. This antecedent-behaviour-consequence contingency is termed the three term contingency. A behaviour which occurs more frequently in the presence of an antecedent condition than in its absence is called a discriminated operant. The antecedent stimulus is called a discriminative stimulus S^D. The fact that the discriminated operant occurs only in the presence of the discriminative stimulus is an illustration of stimulus control.

Measuring Behaviour

When measuring behaviour, there are both dimensions of behaviour and quantifiable measures of behaviour. In applied behaviour analysis, the quantifiable measures are a derivative of the dimensions. These dimensions are repeatability, temporal extent, and temporal locus.

Repeatability

Response classes occur repeatedly throughout time—ie how many times the behaviour occurs.

- **Count** is the number of occurrences in behaviour.
- **Rate/Frequency** is the number of instances of behaviour per unit of time.
- **Celeration** is the measure of how the rate changes over time.

Temporal Extent

This dimension indicates that each instance of behaviour occupies some amount of time—i.e., how long the behaviour occurs.

- **Duration** is the amount of time in which the behaviour occurs.

Temporal Locus

Each instance of behaviour occurs at a specific point in time—i.e., when the behaviour occurs.

- **Response latency** is the measure of elapsed time between the onset of a stimulus and the initiation of the response.

- **Interresponse time** is the amount of time that occurs between two consecutive instances of a response class.

Derivative Measures

Derivative measures are unrelated to specific dimensions:

- **Percentage** is the ratio formed by combining the same dimensional quantities.
- **Trials-to-criterion** are the number of response opportunities needed to achieve a predetermined level of performance.

Analyzing Behaviour Change

Experimental Control

In applied behaviour analysis, all experiments should include the following:

- At least one participant
- At least one behaviour (dependent variable)
- At least one setting
- A system for measuring the behaviour and ongoing visual analysis of data
- At least one treatment or intervention condition
- Manipulations of the independent variable so that its effects on the dependent variable
- An intervention that will benefit the participant in some way

Functional Behaviour Assessment (FBA)

Functional assessment of behaviour provides hypotheses about the relationships between specific environmental events and behaviours. Decades of research has established that both desirable and undesirable behaviours are learned through interactions with the social and physical environment. FBA is used to identify the type and source of reinforcement for challenging behaviours as the basis for intervention efforts designed to decrease the occurrence of these behaviours.

Functions of Behaviour

The function of a behaviour can be thought of as the purpose a behaviour serves for a person. Function is identified in an FBA by identifying the type and source if reinforcement for the behaviour of interest. Those reinforcers might be positive or negative social reinforcers provided by someone who interacts with the person, or automatic reinforcers produced directly by the behaviour itself.

- Positive Reinforcement - social positive reinforcement (attention), tangible reinforcement, and automatic positive reinforcement.
- Negative Reinforcement - social negative reinforcement (escape), automatic negative reinforcement.

Function versus Topography

Behaviours may look different but can serve the same function and likewise behaviour that looks the same may serve multiple functions. What the behaviour looks like often reveals little useful information about the conditions that account for it. However, identifying the conditions that account for a behaviour, suggests what conditions need to be altered to change the behaviour. Therefore, assessment of function of a behaviour can yield useful information with respect to intervention strategies that are likely to be effective.

FBA Methods

FBA methods can be classified into three types:

- Functional (experimental) Analysis
- Descriptive Assessment
- Indirect Assessment

Functional (Experimental) Analysis

A functional analysis is one in which antecedents and consequences are manipulated to indicate their separate effects on the behaviour of interest. This type of arrangement is often called analog because they are not conducted in a naturally occurring context. However, research is indicating that functional analysis done in a natural environment will yield similar or better results

A functional analysis normally has four conditions (three test conditions and one control):

- Contingent attention
- Contingent escape
- Alone
- Control condition

Advantages — It has the ability to yield a clear demonstration of the variable(s)that relate to the occurrence of a problem behaviour. Serves as the standard of scientific evidence by which other assessment alternative are evaluated, and represents the method most often used in research on the assessment and treatment of problem behaviour.

Limitations — Assessment process may temporarily strengthen or increase the undesirable behaviour to unacceptable levels or result in the behaviour acquiring new functions. Some behaviours may not be amenable to functional analysis (e.g. those that, albeit serious, occur infrequently). Functional analysis conducted in contrived settings may not detect the variable that accounts for the occurrence in the natural environment.

Indirect FBA

This method uses structured interviews, checklists, rating scales, or questionnaires to obtain information from persons who are familiar with the person exhibiting the behaviour to identify possible conditions or events in the natural environment that correlate with the problem behaviour. They are called "indirect" because they do not involve direct observation of the behaviour, but rather solicit information based on others' recollections of the behaviour.

- **Advantages** — Some can provide a useful source of information in guiding subsequent, more objective assessments, and contribute to the development of hypotheses about variable that might occasion or maintain the behaviours of concern.
- **Limitations** — Informants may not have accurate and unbiased recall of behaviour and the conditions under which it occurred.

Descriptive FBA

As with Functional Analysis, descriptive functional behaviour assessment utilizes direct observation of behaviour; unlike functional analysis, however, observations are made under naturally occurring conditions. Therefore, descriptive assessments involve observation of the problem behaviour in relation to events that are not arranged in a systematic manner.

There are three variations of descriptive assessment:

- ABC (antecedent-behaviour-consequence) continuous recording — observer records occurrences of targeted behaviour and selected environmental events in the natural routine.
- ABC narrative recording — data are collected only when behaviours of interest are observes, and the recording encompasses any events that immediately precede and follow the target behaviour.
- Scatterplots— a procedure for recording the extent to which a target behaviour occurs more often at particular times than others.

Conducting an FBA

Provided the strengths and limitations of the different FBA procedures, FBA can best be viewed as a four-step process:

1. The gathering of information via indirect and descriptive assessment.
2. Interpretation of information from indirect and descriptive assessment and formulation of a hypothesis about the purpose of problem behaviour.
3. Testing of a hypothesis using a functional analysis.
4. Developing intervention options based on the function of problem behaviour.

Technologies Discovered Through ABA Research

Task Analysis

Task analysis is a process in which a task is analyzed into its component parts so that those parts can be taught through the use of chaining: forward chaining, backward chaining and total task presentation. Task analysis has been used in organizational behaviour management, a behaviour analytic approach to changing organizations. Behavioural scripts often emerge from a task analysis. Bergan conducted a task analysis of the behavioural consultation relationship and Thomas Kratochwill developed a training programme based on teaching Bergan's skills. A similar approach was used for the development of microskills training for counsellors. Ivey would later call this "behaviourist" phase a very productive one and the skills-based approach came to dominate counsellor training during 1970–90. Task analysis was also used in determining the skills needed to access a career. In education, Englemann used task analysis as part of the methods to design the Direct Instruction curriculum.

Chaining

The skill to be learned is broken down into small units for easy learning. For example, a person learning to brush teeth independently may start with learning to unscrew the toothpaste cap. Once they have learned this, the next step may be squeezing the tube, etc.

For problem behaviour, chains can also be analyzed and the chain can be disrupted to prevent the problem behaviour. Some behaviour therapies, such as Dialectical Behaviour Therapy, make extensive use of behaviour chain analysis.

Prompting

A prompt is a cue or assistance to encourage the desired response from an individual. Prompts are often categorized into a prompt hierarchy from most intrusive to least intrusive. There is some controversy about what is considered most intrusive: physically intrusive versus hardest prompt to fade (i.e., verbal). In an errorless learning approach, prompts are given in a most-to-least sequence and faded systematically to ensure the individual experiences a high level of success. There may be instances in which a least-to-most prompt method is preferred. Prompts are faded systematically and as quickly as possible to avoid prompt dependency. The goal of teaching using prompts would be to fade prompts towards independence, so that no prompts are needed for the individual to perform the desired behaviour.

Types of prompts:

- **Verbal prompts:** Utilizing a vocalization to indicate the desired response.
- **Visual Prompts:** a visual cue or picture.
- **Gestural prompts:** Utilizing a physical gesture to indicate the desired response.
- **Positional prompt:** The target item is placed closer to the individual.
- **Modelling:** Modelling the desired response for the student. This type of prompt is best suited for

individuals who learn through imitation and can attend to a model.

- **Physical prompts:** Physically manipulating the individual to produce the desired response. There are many degrees of physical prompts. The most intrusive being hand-over-hand, and the least intrusive being a slight tap to initiate movement.

This is not an exhaustive list of all possible prompts. When using prompts to systematically teach a skill, not all prompts need to be used in the hierarchy; prompts are chosen based on which ones are most effective for a particular individual.

Fading

The overall goal is for an individual to eventually not need prompts. As an individual gains mastery of a skill at a particular prompt level, the prompt is faded to a less intrusive prompt. This ensures that the individual does not become overly dependent on a particular prompt when learning a new behaviour or skill.

Thinning

Thinning is often confused with fading. Fading refers to a prompt being removed, where thinning refers to the spacing of a reinforcement schedule getting larger. Some support exists that a 30% decrease in reinforcement can be an efficient way to thin. Schedule thinning is often an important and neglected issue in contingency management and token economy systems, especially when developed by unqualified practitioners (see professional practice of behaviour analysis).

Generalization

Generalization is the expansion of a student's performance ability beyond the initial conditions set for acquisition of a skill. Generalization can occur across people, places, and materials used for teaching. For example, once a skill is learned in one setting, with a particular instructor, and with specific materials, the skill is taught in more general settings with more variation from the initial acquisition phase. For example, if a student has successfully mastered learning colors at the table, the teacher may take the student around the house or his school and then *generalize* the skill in these more natural environments with other materials. Behaviour analysts have spent considerable amount of time studying factors that lead to generalization.

Shaping

Shaping involves gradually modifying the existing behaviour into the desired behaviour. If the student engages with a dog by hitting it, then he or she could have their behaviour shaped by reinforcing interactions in which he or she touches the dog more gently. Over many interactions, successful shaping would replace the hitting behaviour with patting or other gentler behaviour. Shaping is based on a behaviour analyst's thorough knowledge of operant conditioning principles and Extinction (psychology). Recent efforts to teach shaping have used simulated computer tasks.

Video Modelling

One teaching technique found to be effective with some students, particularly children, is the use of video modelling (the use of taped sequences as exemplars of behaviour). It can be used by therapists to assist in the acquisition of both verbal and motor responses, in some cases for long chains of behaviour.

Interventions Based on an FBA

Critical to behaviour analytic interventions is the concept of a systematic behavioural case formulation with a functional behavioural assessment or analysis at the core. This approach should apply a behaviour analytic theory of change (see behavioral change theories). This formulation should include a thorough functional assessment, a skills assessment, a sequential analysis (behaviour chain analysis), an ecological assessment, a look at existing evidenced-based behavioural models for the problem behaviour (such as Fordyce's model of chronic pain) and then a treatment plan based on how environmental factors influence behaviour. Some argue that behaviour analytic case formulation can be improved with an assessment of rules and rule governed behaviour. Some of the interventions that result from this type of conceptualization involve training specific communication skills to replace the problems behaviour as well as specific setting, antecedent, behaviour, and consequece strategies.

Effectiveness

ABA-based techniques are often used to treat autism, so much so that ABA is often mistakenly considered to be a therapy for autism. ABA-based techniques have demonstrated effectiveness for autism in several controlled studies: children have been shown to make sustained gains in academic performance, adaptive behaviour, and language, with outcomes significantly better than control groups. A 2009 review of educational interventions for children, whose mean age was six years or less at intake, found that the higher-quality studies all assessed ABA, that ABA is well-established and no other educational treatment is considered probably-efficacious, and that intensive ABA treatment, carried out by trained therapists, is demonstrated effective in enhancing global functioning in pre-school children. A 2008 evidence-based review of comprehensive treatment approaches found that ABA is well-established for improving intellectual performance of young children with ASD. A 2009 comprehensive synthesis of early intensive behavioural intervention (EIBI), a form of ABA treatment, found that EIBI produces strong effects, suggesting that it can be effective for some children with autism; it also found that the large effects might be an artifact of comparison groups with treatments that have yet to be empirically validated, and that no comparisons between EIBI and other widely recognized treatment programmes have been published. A 2009 systematic review came to the same principal conclusion that EIBI is effective for some but not all children, with wide variability in response to treatment; it also suggested that any gains are likely to be greatest in the first year of intervention. A 2009 meta-analysis concluded that EIBI has a large effect on full-scale intelligence and a moderate effect on adaptive behaviour. In contrast, when review articles reach the conclusion that ABA-based interventions did not produce significant differences in outcomes, those reviews are found to be based upon incomplete literature reviews and erroneous analyses. For example, a 2009 review and meta-analysis was conducted by two physical therapists who did not have expertise in ABA research methodology. In their article, they reported that applied behaviour intervention (ABI), another name for EIBI, did not significantly improve outcomes compared with standard care of preschool children with ASD in the areas of cognitive outcome, expressive language, receptive language, and adaptive behaviour. However, in a letter to the editor, original source authors pointed out that the literature review ignored key studies, and drew its conclusions based upon only four studies. Further the meta-analysis erroneously identified a treatment group as a control group, which had the effect of increasing the relative success of the control groups in the few studies cited.

●●

8
Virtual Learning Environment

A virtual learning environment **(VLE)** is a software system designed to support teaching and learning in an educational setting, as distinct from a Managed Learning Environment, (MLE) where the focus is on management. A VLE will normally work over the Internet and provide a collection of tools such as those for assessment (particularly of types that can be marked automatically, such as multiple choice), communication, uploading of content, return of students' work, peer assessment, administration of student groups, collecting and organizing student grades, questionnaires, tracking tools, etc. New features in these systems include wikis, blogs, RSS and 3D virtual learning spaces.

While originally created for distance education, VLEs are now most often used to supplement traditional face to face classroom activities, commonly known as Blended Learning. These systems usually run on servers, to serve the course to students Multimedia and/or web pages.

> "Learning is breaking out of the narrow boxes that it was trapped in during the 20th century; teachers' professionalism, reflection and ingenuity are leading learning to places that genuinely excite this new generation of connected young school students — and their teachers too. VLEs are helping to make sure that their learning is not confined to a particular building, or restricted to any single location or moment."

Similar Terms

A VLE is a computer program that facilitates computerized learning or e-learning. Such e-learning systems are sometimes also called Learning Management System (LMS), Content Management System (CMS), Learning Content Management System (LCMS), Managed Learning Environment (MLE), Learning Support System (LSS), Online Learning Centre (OLC), OpenCourseWare (OCW), or Learning Platform (LP); it is education via computer-mediated communication (CMC) or Online Education.

A more correct term may be a virtual environment for learning, rather than virtual learning environment. This removes any ambiguities and identifies that it is the environment which is virtual and not the learning. The term virtual may also contribute to confusion, suggesting that the learning is not real or authentic.

In the United States, CMS and LMS are the more common terms, however LMS is more frequently associated with software for managing corporate training programs rather than courses in traditional education institutions.

In the United Kingdom and many European countries the terms VLE and MLE are favored; however, it is important to realize that these are two very different things. A VLE can be considered a subsystem of an MLE, whereas MLE refers to the wider infrastructure of information systems in an organization that support and enable electronic learning on a wider scale. In fact a rather pedantic reading of the term MLE could be extended to encompass the physical environment in which learning takes place (i.e. a school). Also the use of VLE avoids confusion with the use of LMS to mean "Library Management System".

Becta, in the UK, have coined the term *learning platform* to cover both MLE and VLE as used in the schools sector.

'The term learning platform describes a broad range of ICT systems used to deliver and support learning. Through a learning platform, hardware, software and supporting services are brought together to enable more effective ways of working within and outside the classroom. At the heart of any learning platform is the concept of a personalized online learning space for the pupil. This space should offer teachers and pupils access to stored work, e-learning resources, communication and collaboration with peers, and the facility to track progress.'

Facilities

A VLE should make it possible for a course designer to present to students, through a single, consistent, and intuitive interface, all the components required for a course of education or training. Although logically it is not a requirement, in practice VLEs always make extensive use of computers and the Internet. A VLE should implement all the following elements:

- The syllabus for the course
- Administrative information including the location of sessions, details of pre-requisites and co-requisites, credit information, and how to get help.
- A notice board for up-to-date course information.
- Student registration and tracking facilities, if necessary with payment options.
- Basic teaching materials. These may be the complete content of the course, if the VLE is being used in a distance learning context, or copies of visual aids used in lectures or other classes where it is being used to support a campus-based course.
- Additional resources, including reading materials, and links to outside resources in libraries and on the Internet.

- Self-assessment quizzes which can be scored automatically.
- Formal assessment procedures.
- Electronic communication support including e-mail, threaded discussions and a chat room, with or without a moderator.
- Differential access rights for instructors and students.
- Production of documentation and statistics on the course in the format required for institutional administration and quality control.
- All these facilities should be capable of being hyperlinked together.
- Easy authoring tools for creating the necessary documents including the insertion of hyperlinks — though it is acceptable (arguably, preferable) for the VLE to be designed allowing standard word processors or other office software to be used for authoring.

In addition, the VLE should be capable of supporting numerous courses, so that students and instructors in a given institution (and, indeed, across institutions) experience a consistent interface when moving from one course to another.

Popularity

Universities and other institutions of higher and further education are increasingly turning to VLEs in order to:

- Economize on the time of teaching staff, especially when they are also involved in research and administration. The extent of the economy over traditional "talk-and-chalk" teaching is not yet clear, but for instructors without web development expertise, using a VLE absorbs less time and produces a more professional result.

- Provide a service for students who increasingly look to the internet as the natural medium for finding information and resources.
- Ensure that quality control requirements are met by providing a standard vehicle for collecting the required information.
- Facilitate the integration of distance and campus-based learning or of learning on different campuses.

For example, accredited institutions such as Chapman College University, Touro University, and Adams State College offer online, on-demand teacher training courses for educators to earn graduate credit and/or masters degrees. In the UK schools are being encouraged to make use of learning platforms. The DCSF in the UK government has published an eStrategy outlining priorities that include every learner in schools having access to an online learning space and e-portfolio.

Transferring Course Content

Most VLEs support Shareable Content Object Reference Model (SCORM) as a standard way to upload, launch and track courses. There are no commonly used standards that define how the learner's performance within a course should be transferred from one VLE to another.

Some institutions have attempted to combat this problem by agreeing to share common platforms. Use of open source VLEs such as Moodle (moodle is also referred to as a CMS or Course Management System) have more recently enabled institutions to share content more easily. For the schools sector in the UK the DCSF via Becta has defined a learning platform "conformance framework" to encourage interoperability.

Systems Available

For those wishing to deliver e-learning there are many free open source and proprietary VLEs available for use. On-demand e-learning services are also a popular choice because they can be deployed in minutes and don't require instructors & institutions to run their own servers.

Many VLEs are placed on a web server. In a typical VLE there are one or more programmes or languages that provides the user (Teacher-Student) interface, and which interacts with a database. For example, a VLE might use PHP as its web language/program, with MySQL as a database.

VLEs are increasingly found in new niches. These include new emerging technologies, as well as specialized markets. A VLE can be deployed on a USB drive as a child, which synchronizes from time to time with its web based parent. VLEs can be used for training or in something as specialized as to meet ISO 9000 certification requirements.

Virtual World Learning Environments

Emerging technologies include Sloodle, a merge of Second Life, Moodle, i.e. integrating virtual worlds and course management . This early development approach hints at new options for enabling learning in a social, immersive, and interactive way. Another 3D virtual learning environment called Edusim brings a lessons driven 3D virtual environment to the classroom interactive whiteboard surface allowing the direct manipulation of 3D virtual objects. Umgumbo is an immersive 3D VLE set in a Newtonian simulation of the solar system. Still in development, Umgumbo will allow collaborative and interactive learning within personalized 3D spaces, including educational gaming, and is delivered from a single external website.

List of some Virtual Learning Environments

Learning Management Systems

- Claroline
- Desire2Learn
- eFront — An Open-Source web-based Learning Management System
- JoomlaLMS — a LMS based on Joomla platform
- LAMS — the Learning Activity Management System
- SharePointLMS — a LMS based on MS SharePoint
- TotalLMS

Course Management Systems

- CCNet
- Coggno - e-learning software platform and courseware creation toolkit
- Desire2Learn
- Pegasus LMS Pearson Publications

Free software and open source

- Dokeos
- ILIAS
- Moodle
- Sakai

Virtual Learning Environment

- Blackboard — A family of virtual learning software
- CyberExtension — Virtual Managed Learning Environment
- Desire2Learn — Desire2Learn eLearning solutions

- FirstClass — Messaging and communications solution
- Heritage Key — Virtual historical environments, such as Tutankhamun's tomb.
- It's Learning — Norwegian Closed Source System (written in ASP.NET)
- WebCT — (Now a part of Blackboard) Software applications designed to enhance teaching and learning
- WebTrain — Virtual live classes, enrollment, attendance, attention monitoring.

Other Descriptions

- Apex Learning — K-12 online course service and AP test study
- ATutor — LCMS
- Dokeos — elearning and course management web application
- eCollege — comprehensive eLearning solution
- Pass-port — a commercial ePortfolio and assessment system that includes a course management component
- Spiral Universe — student information system
- Yacapaca — free assessment platform with large repository of User-generated content

VIRTUAL SCHOOL

A **virtual school** or **cyberschool** describes an institution that teaches courses entirely or primarily through online methods. Though there are tens of thousands of commercial and non-accredited courses available online, the term "virtual school" is generally reserved for accredited schools that teach a full-time (or nearly full-time) course of instruction designed to lead to a degree. Virtual public and private schools serving every grade level including graduate programs may elect to pursue accreditation through various regional and national organizations. Accredited schools must meet rigorous standards as defined by the issuing organization and are designed to insure that students are receiving the highest quality instruction and education.

All student services are conducted through Internet technology. The virtual school differ/contrasts from the traditional school through the physical media that links administrators, teachers and students and is an alliance of public distance learning schools. Many states in the United States have their own virtual school, and many of them have students numbering in the thousands. By providing a student's social security number the person is then entered into a database where they can choose which classes they want to take.

There are many different virtual school instructional and enrollment models. Instructional models range from fully independent self paced courses to semester based, teacher facilitated courses. Class sizes range widely with anywhere from 25 students to as many as 200 students in each class section. Students keep in contact with teachers and collaborate with other students through web communication tools provided in the course delivery platforms like Blackboard or Desire2Learn or Moodle . In some cases students communicate by phone with instructors. To help with communication many virtual schools have implemented their own system programs to help build courses and maintain student profiles. There are also many books and training manuals to aid in the development of such schools and courses.

Many of today's virtual schools are descendants of correspondence schools. Sometimes referred to as "distance learning," correspondence schools offered students an alternative to the traditional brick and mortar meetings within a schoolhouse. These schools utilized the postal service for student-teacher interaction, or used two-way radio transmissions, sometimes with pre-recorded television broadcasts. Students were expected to study their learning material independently and, in some cases, meet with a proctor to be tested. Modern virtual schools provide similar alternatives to students with a more ubiquitous and, often, interactive approach.

Virtual Schools now exist all around the world. Some of these virtual schools have been integrated into public schools (particularly in the United States), where students sit in computer labs and do their work online. In other situations, students can be completely homeschooled, or they can take any combination of public/private/homeschooling and online classes.

Pricing and Location

Virtual schools may be free if the state pays for the courses, otherwise, there will be a course fee to be paid for by the student, parents or student's home school. Other materials would be purchased by the student, such as books.

Materials can also add up. Most courses will provide electronic materials free of cost, but others require some shopping on the students part. Textbooks are not required but can be used as an aid for coursework.

Materials

As mentioned earlier, many materials are provided free of cost. Some schools provide programmes, usually for web design classes. Some popular materials include Adobe Systems products, Jasc products, and products from Macromedia. Other schools may use Corel products as a cheaper alternative. These products are usually free. Student usually receiceves the full version of the selected programme, with a limited license, usually 1 year or so. These programmes are key in the success of virtual schools, and help them to improve each year. Many schools will also provide a brand new computer for all students in need of one. Generally, these computers run using the Microsoft operating system, Windows XP, but depending on lesson needs and coursework the school may also use Linux based computers or Apple Macintoshes.

Advantages and Disadvantages

Advocates of virtual learning believe that virtual schools hold advantages including: not being required to attend and travel to face-to-face classes and the integration digital media into the curricula. Some virtual schools include online study groups in which students interact with each other online.

Unlike traditional education delivery methods, students at virtual schools do not directly interact with professors. Hence, virtual education is considered by many to be equivalent to a directed-learning programme. Because students do not interact with their instructors or peers face-to-face, "lack of socialization" is often quoted, as a disadvantage by detractors. Recent anecdotal evidence provided by one virtual school from one live cyberschool indicates that, while socialization may be different, it is not necessarily lacking. It is also recommended that students enrolled in virtual schools be involved in social activities outside school, much like homeschooled children.

Many students are drawn to online learning for a variety of reasons; particularly, the ability to avoid the requirement of traveling to a physical location, which may be impossible for some non-traditional learners. Critics argue that for online education to be taken seriously, online programmes must adhere to generally accepted educational standards. To reduce this criticism. A virtual learning organization has developed a set of standards released on February 21, 2008. Some believe that this is an important first step in monitoring online programmes, but it should be noted that while every provider of education must be accredited, the quality of accreditation varies significantly. For instance, the non-profit AACSB is the most prestigious accreditation agency for business schools and no virtual schools have received accreditation by the agency.

VIRTUAL EDUCATION

Virtual education refers to instruction in a learning environment where teacher and student are separated by time or space, or both, and the teacher provides course content through course management applications, multimedia resources, the Internet, videoconferencing, etc. Students receive the content and communicate with the teacher via the same technologies.

Characteristics of Virtual Education

Virtual education is a term describing online education using the Internet. This term is primarily used in higher education where so-called Virtual Universities have been established.

Virtual courses – a synonym is online courses – are courses delivered on the Internet. "Virtual" is used here to characterize the fact that the course is not taught in a classroom face-to-face but through some substitute mode that can be associated with classroom teaching.

A virtual programme (or a virtual course of studies) is a study program in which all courses or at least a significant portion of the courses are virtual courses.

Instruction Modes for Virtual Education

Many virtual study programmes are mainly text based, using HTML, PowerPoint, or PDF documents. Multimedia technologies have been investigated for many years and eventually found their way into practice. Today a wide spectrum of instruction modes is available, including the following:

- *Virtual Classroom:* A virtual classroom is a learning environment created in the virtual space. The objectives of a virtual classroom are to improve access to advanced educational experiences by allowing students and instructors to participate in remote learning communities using personal computers; and to improve the quality and effectiveness of education by using the computer to support a collaborative learning process. The explosion of the knowledge age has changed the context of what is learnt and how it is learnt – the concept of virtual classrooms is a manifestation of this knowledge revolution.

- *Hypertext courses:* Structured course material is used as in a conventional distance education program. However, all material is provided electronically and can be viewed with a browser. Hyperlinks connect text, multimedia parts and exercises in a meaningful way.

- *Video-based courses* are like face-to-face classroom courses, with a lecturer speaking and Powerpoint slides or online examples used for illustration. Video-streaming technologies is used. Students watch the video by means of freeware or plug-ins (e.g. Windows Media Player, RealPlayer).

- *Audio-based courses* are similar but instead of moving pictures only the sound track of the lecturer is provided. Often the course pages are enhanced with a text transcription of the lecture.

- *Animated courses:* Enriching text-oriented or audio-based course material by animations is generally a good way of making the content and its appearance more interesting. Animations are created using Macromedia

Flash or similar technologies. These animations help understand key concepts and also allow for better retention of learning.

- *Web-supported textbook courses* are based on specific textbooks. Students read and reflect the chapters by themselves. Review questions, topics for discussion, exercises, case studies, etc. are given chapterwise on a website and discussed with the lecturer. Class meetings may be held to discuss matters in a chatroom, for example.
- *Peer-to-peer courses* are courses taught "on-demand" and without a prepared curriculum. A new field of online education has emerged in 2007 through new online education platforms.

Communication and Interaction

Students in virtual education typically acquire knowledge in a uni-directional manner first (e.g. by studying a video, reading a textbook chapter). Subsequent discussions of problems, solving exercises, case studies, review questions, etc. help the students to understand better what they learned before. Electronic media like a discussion forum, chat room, voice mail, e-mail, etc. are often employed for communication.

Homework assignments are normally submitted electronically, e.g. as an attachment to an e-mail. When help is needed, lecturers, tutors, or fellow students, or a help desk are available, just like in a real university. The difference is that all communication goes via electronic media.

9
Virtual University

The term **"virtual university"** is used to describe any organization that provides higher education programmes through electronic devices such as the computer or a TV Screen. Some of the Universities are real institutes, the bricks and mortar type that provide online learning as part of their extended university courses while others provide courses only on-line.

Some of these organizations exist only as loosely tied combines of universities, institutes or departments that together provide a number of courses over the Internet, television or other media, that are separate and distinct from programs offered by the single institution outside of the combine. Others are actual organizations with a legal framework, yet named virtual because they appear only on the internet, without a physical location aside from administration units. Still other virtual universities can be organized through specific or multiple physical locations, with some having actual campuses to receive programme delivery through technological media that is broadcast from another location, where real professors give televised lectures.

The goal of Virtual Universities is to provide access to that part of the population who would not be able to attend a physical campus, for reasons such as: (1) distance — where students live too far from a physical campus to attend regular classes; (2) need for flexibility – some students need the flexibility to study at home whenever it is convenient for them to do so.

Program delivery in a virtual university is administered through information communication technology such as web pages, e-mail and other networked sources. When the term "virtual" was first coined in the computational sense, it applied to things that were simulated by the computer like virtual memory. Over time, the adjective has been applied to things that really exist and are created or carried on by means of computers.

Students taking so called "virtual" courses are doing "real" work to get their degrees and educators preparing and teaching those courses spend plenty of "real" time in doing so. That is, students meet rigorous academic learning outcomes and evaluations through programmes constructed by credible academics according to standard university-level criteria. Many Virtual Universities are accredited in the same way as traditional universities and operate according to the same academic standards. These universities can grant degrees that will be recognized around the world. Online programmes can be marketed to any person who has on-line access to provide learning experiences and training in an open access format.

History of Virtual Universities

Before the advent of Virtual Universities most higher education institutes offered some distance education which consisted of print-based correspondence courses. These courses were often referred to as a "course in a box". Whenever a student signed up for a course through distance education, they would receive a package from the university that included all of the materials that they would need for the course. There are still courses being offered this way and most universities have distance education or continuing education departments. The downside to the old correspondence courses was that if a student had a question or a problem then they had to rely on the regular mail to get their answers. This could involve weeks of waiting for a reply. The good news is that today, students who study through correspondence like courses can get almost immediate feedback from professors and online tutors through e-mails or online discussions. The defining characteristic of all forms and generations of distance education is the separation of student and teacher in time and space. Distance education can be seen as the precursor to online learning.

The Open University in the United Kingdom was the world's first successful distance teaching university. It was founded in the 1960's on the belief that communications technology could bring high quality degree-level learning to people who had not had the opportunity to attend campus universities The idea for a "wireless university" was first discussed at the BBC (British Broadcasting Corporation) by the educationalist and historian J.C. Stobbart. From these early beginnings more ideas came forth until finally the Labour Party under the leadership of Harold Wilson formed an advisory committee to establish an Open University.

With the goal of bringing higher education to all those who wanted to access it, the committee came up with various scenarios before settling on the name Open University. The first idea floated in the UK was to have a "teleuniversity" which would combine broadcast lectures with correspondence texts and visits to conventional universities. In the "teleuniversity" scenario courses are taught on the radio and television and in fact many universities adopted the use of this technology for their distance education courses. The name "teleuniversity" morphed into the "University of Air" which still had the same goal of reaching the lower income groups who did not have access to higher education. The name "University of Air" did not stick and by the time the first students were admitted in January 1971 the name had become what it is today "Open University". OU proved that it was possible to teach university-level courses to students at a distance.

By 1980, total students numbers at OU had reached 70,000 and some 6,000 people were graduating each year. The 1980's saw increased expansion continue as more courses and subject areas were introduced; as the importance of career development grew, so the university began to offer professional training courses alongside its academic programmes. By the mid-nineties the OU was using the internet. Today (2008) more that 180,000 students are interacting with the OU online from home.

The idea of a virtual university as an institution that used computers and telecommunications instead of buildings and transport to bring students and teachers together for university courses was first published in 1995 by John Tiffin and Lalita Rajasingham in their book "In Search of the Virtual Class: Education in an Information Society" (London and New York, Routledge). It was based on a joint research project at Victoria University of Wellington that ran from 1986-1996. Called the the virtual class laboratory, it used dedicated telecommunication systems to make it possible for students to attend class virtually or physically and was at first supported by a number of telecommunication organizations. Its purpose was to seek the critical factors in using ICT for university level education. In 1992 the virtual class lab moved onto the Internet and in 1995 The Open University of Catalonia became the first virtual university totally dependent on telecommunications and computers.

A number of other universities were involved in the late eighties in pioneering initiatives and experiments were conducted between Victoria University in New Zealand, the University of Hawaii, Ohio State University and Waseda University to try and conduct classes and courses at an international level via telecommunications. This led to the concept of a Global Virtual University (Tiffin and Rajasingham (2003)"The Global Virtual University" London and New York, Routledge).

Studying in a Virtual University

The convenience of on-line learning attracts mainly working class adult students who need school to meet their schedules and demands of working, family and social lives.

Providing access to Higher Education for all students, especially adult learners, is made easier by the fact that most Virtual Universities have no entry requirements for their undergraduate courses. Entry requirements are needed for the courses that are aimed at postgraduates or those who work in specific jobs.

Studying in a virtual university is different from studying in a brick and mortar university. There are no buildings and no campus to go to because students study on the internet. In most cases, only a personal computer and an Internet connection is needed.

If you are taking courses on-line it means that you will be learning in your own time by reading course material, working on course activities, writing assignments and perhaps working with other students through interactive teleconferences. Online learning can be an isolating experience since the student spends the majority of their time working by themselves. Some learners do not mind learning by themselves but others find this a major stumbling block to successful completion of courses. Course materials can include printed material, books, audio and video cassettes, TV programmes, cd-rom /software, and web sites. Support is offered to learners from the professor or a tutor online through e-mails if they are having problems with the course.

It is often difficult to maintain the scheduling needed to be successful when learning on-line. That is why some Virtual Universities apply the same type of time management as traditional schools. Many courses operate to a timetable, which the student receives with his/her course materials.

These include the planned activities for each week of the course and the dates for the assignments. If the course has an exam, the students will be informed where they have to go to write it.

An example of a university that maintains a tight schedule is the Virtual Global University (VGU) in Germany. VGU offers a graduate programme "International Master of Business Informatics" (MBI) – a master program in information technology and management that takes four semesters to complete (full-time students). Each course has a lecture or a virtual class meeting every week. Afterwards, students get a homework assignment; for example, they have to solve an exercise, elaborate on some problem, discuss a case study, or take a test. Lecturers give them immediate feedback, and one week later, the same happens again.

Teaching Modes

When on-line courses first began the primary mode of delivery was through a two way audio/video network. Then as well as now, many of the virtual study programmes were/are mainly based on text documents, but multimedia technologies have become increasingly popular as well. These web-based delivery modes are used in order to expand access to programmes and services that can be offered anytime and anywhere. The spectrum of teaching modes in virtual education includes courses based on hypertext, videos, audios, e-mails, video conferencing. Teaching on the web through courseware such as WebCT and BlackBoard are also used. See Virtual education.

Concern of On-Line Learning

There are a great many skills that students who decide to study through Virtual Universities need in order to be successful. Some of these include:

- Mastering software tools,
- Developing new study habits,

- Knowing how to access on line academic resources,
- Confidence to do well. Students who lack self-confidence, often have poor learning skills and may develop considerable anxiety and fear of failure,
- Students need to be highly motivated and be able to learn on their own without much direction,
- Need excellent time management skills to ensure that they get the work completed when it is due,
- Ability to Ask for Help. Services for students often include tutorials between student-tutor, and student-student, help desks, counselling and advising plus technical support. However, just providing these services does not guarantee success.

Quality of On-Line Universities

With the rapid expansion in the past ten years of Virtual Universities questions remain about accreditation, assessment and reputation for quality. Not all Virtual Universities are created equal. Accreditation, by a governing body, is needed to assure students that the online institute has certified online instructors who have the expertise and educational qualifications to design and carry out the curriculum. As well assessment needs to be closely monitored in any institution but especially in Virtual Universities. Without assessment there would be no measure to determine levels of current knowledge or whether the learning objective was accomplished. Reputation for quality is important because employers will be more likely to hire a student who got their degree online from an accredited university with a good name than one no one has heard of. Vicky Philips, CEO of Geteducated.com, says "The issue is not whether the degree is earned at a distance, but whether or not the student is familiar with the name of the institution granting the degree, the name takes precedence over the method". Philips clarifies this by saying, "respondents in studies of opinions about online degrees will rate a degree from Stanford the same whether it's earned online or on-campus, because they recognize the name of the institution granting the degree."

ONLINE DEGREES

The term **online degrees** refers to college degrees that can be earned primarily or entirely through the use of an Internet-connected computer, rather than attending college in a traditional campus setting. Improvements in technology and the increasing use of the Internet worldwide have led to a proliferation of online colleges that award associate's, bachelor's, master's and doctoral degrees.

Accreditation

The goal of educational accreditation, according to the U.S. Department of Education, is to ensure that programmes provided by institutions of higher education meet acceptable levels of quality. In the area of online education, it is important to avoid diploma mills that offer fake degrees at a cost. Students seeking valid online degrees should **obtain proof of accreditation** from a regional or national/specialized accrediting body in the United States. Online colleges that are fully accredited have earned a widely recognized form of university accreditation from one of six regional accreditation boards.

Each of the six geographic regions of the United States has a non-governmental, regional agency that oversees and accredits degree-granting institutions headquartered in their areas. There are six regional accreditation boards:

- Middle States Association of Colleges and Schools
- Northwest Commission on Colleges and Universities
- North Central Association of Colleges and Schools
- New England Association of Schools and Colleges

- Southern Association of Colleges and Schools
- Western Association of Schools & Colleges

The Department of Education and the Council for Higher Education Accreditation (CHEA) recognize the Distance Education and Training Council (DETC) as the accrediting organization for distance learning institutions and education programmes that offer online degrees.

Quality of Learning Online

Online education is a proven model for learning, with a lengthy track record. It enables accredited higher learning for individuals living with physical disabilities, busy working class people, soldiers and those living abroad, and stay at home parents to mention a few. There is fundamentally little difference between physically sitting in an auditorium listening to lectures versus watching a webcasted video of the professor.

The recognition of the quality of online degrees compared to on-campus degrees varies. While most major online colleges are regionally accredited, the public perception of their quality is in dispute. Some experts argue that degrees in certain fields are more accepted online than in others, while some programs are less suited for online-only schools.

A survey by the Distance Education and Training Council found that 100 percent of employers who responded felt that distance education programme graduates performed better on the job as a result of their degree (as compared to their previous performance). Additionally, employers felt that an employee receiving a distance education degree compared favourably, in terms of knowledge learned, to someone with a resident degree.

In some instances, an online degree may be no different than a degree earned in a campus-based programme. The instruction is often exactly the same, and the online degree contains no special designation.

OPEN UNIVERSITY

The Open University (commonly **Open University** or **OU**, but officially "the" is part of its name) is the distance learning university founded and funded by the UK Government. It is notable for having an open entry policy, i.e. students' previous academic achievements are not taken into account for entry to most undergraduate courses. The majority of undergraduate students are based in the United Kingdom, but its courses can be studied anywhere in the world.. Most of the postgraduate students are based on campus where they take courses and attend the OU facilities for research.

It was established in 1969. It is incorporated by Royal Charter as an exempt charity in England and Wales and a registered charity in Scotland.

The administration is based at Walton Hall, Milton Keynes in Buckinghamshire, but has regional centres in each of its thirteen regions around the UK. It also has offices in other European countries. The University awards undergraduate and postgraduate degrees, as well as non-degree qualifications such as diplomas and certificates, or continuing education units.

With more than 180,000 students enrolled, including more than 25,000 students studying overseas, it is the largest academic institution in the UK by student number, and qualifies as one of the world's largest universities. Since it was founded, more than 3 million students have studied its courses. It was rated top university in England and Wales for student satisfaction in the 2005 and 2006 UK government national student satisfaction survey, and second in the 2007 survey.

Aims

The OU provides university education to those wishing to pursue higher education on a part-time and/or distance learning basis, including disabled people, who are officially a priority group for the university. The British Government asked the Open University to continue the work of the Council for National Academic Awards (CNAA) when it was dissolved. The CNAA formerly awarded degrees at the polytechnics which have since become universities.

Foundation

The Open University was founded by the Labour government of Harold Wilson, based on the vision of Michael Young (later Lord Young of Dartington). Planning commenced in 1965 under Minister of State for Education Jennie Lee, who led an advisory committee consisting of university vice-chancellors, educationalists and broadcasters. The BBC's Assistant Director of Engineering at the time, James Redmond had obtained most of his qualifications at night school, and his natural enthusiasm for the project did much to overcome the technical difficulties of using television to broadcast teaching programmes.

Walter Perry (later Lord Perry) was appointed the OU's first vice-chancellor in January 1969, and its Foundation Secretary was Anastasios Christodoulou. The election of the new Conservative government of Edward Heath in 1970 led to budget cuts under Chancellor of the Exchequer Iain Macleod (who had earlier called the idea of an Open University "blithering nonsense").

However the OU accepted its first 25,000 students in 1971, adopting a radical open admissions policy. At the time, the total "traditional" university population in the UK was around 130,000.

Students

People from all walks of life and all ages take advantage of the OU; for most courses there are no entry requirements other than the ability to study at an appropriate level, though most postgraduate courses require evidence of previous study or equivalent life experience.

Approximately 70% of students are in full-time employment, often working towards a first (or additional) degree or qualification to progress or change their career, with over 50,000 being sponsored by their employer. The University is also popular with those who cannot physically attend a traditional university because they are disabled, abroad, in prison, serving in the armed forces, or looking after family members. About 10,000 OU students have disabilities.

While most of those studying are mature students, the reduction in financial support for those attending traditional universities has also led to an influx of young undergraduates to the OU.

In the 2003–2004 academic year, around 20% of undergraduates were under 25 years old, up from 12.5% in 1996–1997 (the year before top-up fees were announced) and a small minority are under 18. The OU works with some schools to introduce A Level students to OU study.

Unlike other universities, where students register for a programme, at the OU students register separately for individual modules (which may be 10, 15, 20, 30 or 60 CATS points, equivalent to 5, 7.5, 10, 15, or 30 ECTS credits), and are known as 'courses' in the OU context. These courses may then be linked into degree programmes.

The students' union is the Open University Students Association, usually abbreviated to OUSA.

Staff

The majority of staff are Associate Lecturers and, as of the 2006-2007 academic year, there are over eight thousand working for OU. There are also 1,218 salaried academic employees, 1,654 others who are also academic-related, and 1,847 support staff (including secretaries and technicians).

Teaching Methods

The OU uses a variety of methods for distance learning, including written and audio materials, the Internet, disc-based software and television programmes on DVD. Course-based television broadcasts by the BBC, which started on 3 January 1971, ceased on 15 December 2006. Materials are composed of originally-authored work by in-house and external academic contributors, and from third-party materials licensed for use by OU students. For most courses, students are supported by tutors ("Associate Lecturers") who provide feedback on their work and are generally available to them at face-to-face tutorials, by telephone, and/or on the Internet. A number of short courses worth ten points are now available that do not have an assigned tutor but offer an online conferencing service (Internet Forum) where help and advice is offered through conferencing "Moderators".

Some courses have mandatory day schools. These are day-long sessions which a student must attend in order to pass the course. One example of such a course is the K301 - Advanced Certificate in Health Promotion - which has two mandatory day schools/workshops, focusing on communication skills, counselling and practical issues related to health promotion. Nevertheless, it is possible to seek excusal upon the basis of ill-health (or other extenuating circumstances), and many courses have no mandatory face-to-face component.

Similarly, many courses have traditionally offered week

long summer schools offering an opportunity for students to remove themselves from the general distractions of their life and focus on their study for a short time.

Over the past ten years the University has adopted a policy of separating residential courses from distance-taught courses. Exemption from attendance at residential schools, always as an Alternative Learning Experience (ALE), is sometimes available for disabled students and others who find it impossible to attend in person.

The OU now produces mainstream television and radio programming aimed at bringing learning to a wider audience. Most of this programming, including series such as *Rough Science* and "Battle of the Geeks", are broadcast at peak times, while older programming is carried in the BBC Learning Zone.

In October 2006 the OU joined the Open educational resources movement with the launch of OpenLearn. A growing selection of current and past distance learning course materials will be released for free access, including downloadable versions for educators to modify (under the Creative Commons BY-NC-SA licence), plus free collaborative learning-support tools.

Assessment Methods

The Open University offers courses that are generally assessed using an equal weighting of examinations and coursework. The coursework component normally takes the form of between two and six tutor marked assignments (TMAs) and, occasionally, may also include up to six multiple-choice or "missing word" 100-question computer marked assignments (CMAs). The examinable component is usually a proctored three hour paper regardless of the course size (although on some courses it can be up to three three-hour papers), but may also be an ECA (End of Course Assessment) which is similar to a TMA, in that it is completed at home, but is regarded as an exam for grading purposes. Course results are sometimes issued on a graded basis, consisting of pass grades 1 (threshold 85%,a distinction), 2 (70-84%), 3 (55-69%) & 4 (40-54%), and fail (below 40%). This grade is calculated as the lower of the overall continuous assessment score (OCAS) and overall examination score (OES).

These grades can be weighted according to their level, and combined to calculate the classification of a degree. An undergraduate degree will weight level 3 courses twice as much as level 2, and in postgraduate programmes all M level courses are equally weighted.

Qualifications

Undergraduate

Open University courses have associated with them a number of Credit Accumulation and Transfer Scheme (CATS) points — usually 30 or 60 — depending on the quantity of the material in the course and a level (1, 2, 3, or 4) corresponding to the complexity, with 120 points roughly equating to the year of study for a full time student.

The OU offers a large number of undergraduate qualifications, including certificates, diplomas, and Bachelors degrees, based on both level and quantity of study. An OU undergraduate degree requires 300 (or 360 for honours) CATS points.

Students generally do not undertake more than 60 points per year, meaning that an undergraduate degree will take typically six years to complete. With the exception of some degrees in fast moving areas (such as computing) there is generally no limit on the time which a student may take. Students need special permission to take more than 120 points (equivalent to full-time study) at any time; such permission is not usually granted.

Originally BA was the only undergraduate degree, and it was unnamed. The modern OU grants both BA and BSc undergraduate degrees, and they may be named (following a specified syllabus) or unnamed (constructed of courses chosen by the student).

Many OU faculties have now introduced short courses worth ten points. Most of these courses are taught online, and start at regular intervals throughout the year. They typically provide an introduction to a broader subject over a period of ten weeks, these are generally timed during vacations at conventional universities in order to take advantage of their facilities. Some science courses, which require only home study, are complemented by residential courses, in order to allow the student to gain practical laboratory experience in that field; typically, an award of degree or diploma will require completion of both.

Different courses are run at different times of the year, but, typically, a 30 or 60 point course will run from February through to October. Assessment is by both continual assessment (with, normally, between four and eight assignments during the year) and, for most, a final examination or on some courses a major assignment.

Degrees

As well as degrees in named subject, the Open University also grants "open" Bachelor degrees where the syllabus is designed by the students by combining any number of Open University courses up to 360 credits for an open honours degree — the main restriction on which courses can be included is that there must be at least 120 at level 3 and no more than 120 at level 1.

Other Qualifications

The Open University grants undergraduate **Certificates** (abbreviated Cert) typically awarded after 60 completed credits at Level 1 or Level 3 (where each credit corresponds to roughly 10 hours of study, therefore 60 credits represent about 600 hours of effort), **Diplomas** (abbreviated Dip) after 120 credits — typically 60 points at Level 2 and 60 points at Level 3, ordinary **Bachelor degrees** (abbreviated BA, BSc, etc) after 300 credits, and **Bachelor degrees with honours**, (abbreviated BA (Hons), BSc (Hons), etc) after 360 credits. Open University also awards **Foundation degrees** (abbreviated FdA, FdSc, etc).

Postgraduate

The Open University provides the opportunity to study for a PhD on a part time distance, or a full time on site basis in a wide range of disciplines as well as an EdD for professionals in education. The University also offers a range of Master's levels courses such as the MBA and MPA, MSc, MA and MEd, and MRes, as well as the professional PGCE qualification and a number of postgraduate diplomas and certificates including innovative practice-based courses and postgraduate computing qualifications for professionals. Postgraduate certificates are awarded for 60 points of study on specified courses; postgraduate diplomas are awarded for 120 points of study on specified courses. The University offers "Advanced Diplomas" that involve 60 credits at undergraduate level and 60 credits at postgraduate level - these are designed as "bridges" between undergraduate and postgraduate study.

Academic Divisions

Faculties

The University has Faculties of Arts, Education & Language Studies, Health & Social Care, Law, Mathematics, Computing and Technology, Science, Social Science, and a Business School. There is no School of Medicine. The new Faculty of Mathematics, Computing and Technology was formed on 1 October 2007.

Business School

The OU Business School is the largest provider of MBAs in the UK, producing more graduates than all the rest of the business schools in the UK put together. Its courses are recognised by AMBA, EQUIS, AACSB, and CEL.

Although the majority of students at the Business School are in the UK, many of the courses are also available throughout most of the world. Students study via distance learning for a Certificate or Diploma in Management and MBA programmes. A number of courses have compulsory residential school which students must attend. The faculty also offers Honours and Foundation degrees in Business Studies and Leadership & Management.

The first Diploma courses were developed from 1983; however the School did not become a separate entity until 1988, when development of the first MBA courses was started. The first MBA students were enrolled in 1989, and the School almost immediately became the largest business school in Europe.

Research

Like other UK universities, the OU actively engages in research. The OU's Planetary and Space Sciences Research Institute has become particularly well known to the public through its involvement in space missions. In October 2006, the Cassini-Huygens mission including 15 people from the OU received the 2006 "Laurels for Team Achievement Award" from the International Academy of Astronautics (IAA). Cassini-Huygens' successful completion of its seven-year, two billion-mile journey in January 2005 to Saturn ended with Huygens landing farther away from Earth than any previous probe or craft in the history of space exploration. The first instrument to touch Saturn's moon Titan was the *Surface Science Package* containing nine sensors to investigate the physical properties of Titan's surface. It was built by a team at the OU led by Professor John Zarnecki.

10
Educational Software

Educational software is computer software, the primary purpose of which is teaching or self-learning.

Early History, 1940s—1970s

The use of computer hardware and software in education and training dates to the early 1940s, when American researchers developed flight simulators which used analog computers to generate simulated onboard instrument data. One such system was the type19 synthetic radar trainer, built in 1943. From these early attempts in the WWII era through the mid 1970s, educational software was directly tied to the hardware, usually mainframe computers, on which it ran. Pioneering educational computer systems in this era included the PLATO system (1960), developed at the University of Illinois, and TICCIT (1969). In 1963, IBM had established a partnership with Stanford University's Institute for Mathematical Studies in the Social Sciences (IMSSS), directed by Patrick Suppes, to develop the first comprehensive CAI elementary school curriculum which was implemented on a large scale in schools in both California and Mississippi. In 1967 Computer Curriculum Corporation (CCC, now Pearson Education Technologies) was formed to market to schools the materials developed through the IBM partnership. Early terminals that ran educational systems cost over $10,000, putting them out of reach of most institutions. Some programming languages from this period, particularly BASIC (1963), and LOGO (1967) can also be considered educational, as they were specifically targeted to students and novice computer users. The PLATO IV system, released in 1972, supported many features which later became standard in educational software running on home computers. Its features included bitmap graphics, primitive sound generation, and support for non-keyboard input devices, including the touchscreen.

History 1970s – 1980s

The arrival of the personal computer, with the altair 8800 in 1975, changed the field of software in general, with specific implications for educational software. Whereas users prior to 1975 were dependent upon university or government owned mainframe computers with timesharing, users after this shift could create and use software for computers in homes and schools, computers available for less than $2000. By the early 1980s, the availability of personal computers including the Apple II (1977), Commodore PET (1977), Commodore VIC-20 (1980), and Commodore 64 (1982) allowed for the creation of companies and nonprofits which specialized in educational software. Brøderbund and the Learning Company are key companies from this period, and MECC, the Minnesota Educational Computing Consortium, a key non-profit software developer. These and other companies designed a range of titles for personal computers, with the bulk of the software initially developed for the Apple II.

History 1990s

Major developments in educational software in the early and mid 1990s were made possible by advances in computer hardware. Multimedia graphics and sound were increasingly used in educational programs. CD-ROMs became the preferred method for content delivery. With the spread of the internet in the second half of the 1990s, new methods of educational software delivery appeared. In the history of virtual learning environments, the 1990s were a time of growth for educational software systems, primarily due to the advent of the affordable computer and of the Internet. Today, Higher Education institutions use virtual learning environments like Blackboard Inc. to provide greater accessibility to learners.

Major Types of Educational Software

Children's Learning and Home Learning

An immense number of titles, probably running into the thousands, were developed and released from the mid-1990's onwards, aimed primarily at the home education of younger children. Later iterations of these titles often began to link educational content to school curricula (such as England's National Curriculum). The design of educational software programmes for home use has been influenced strongly by computer gaming concepts – in other words, they are designed to be fun as well as educational. However as far as possible a distinction should be drawn between proper learning titles (such as these) and software where the gaming outweighs the educational value.

The following are examples of children's learning software which have a structured pedagogical approach, usually orientated towards literacy and numeracy skills.

- Disney Interactive learning titles based on characters such as Winnie-the-Pooh, Aladdin, The Jungle Book and Mickey Mouse
- GCompris, contains numerous activities, from computer discovery to science
- Knowledge Adventure's JumpStart and Blaster Learning System series
- The Learning Company's Reader Rabbit, The ClueFinders and Zoombinis series

Courseware

Courseware is a term that combines the words 'course' with 'software'. Its meaning originally was used to describe additional educational material intended as kits for teachers or trainers or as tutorials for students, usually packaged for use with a computer. The term's meaning and usage has expanded and can refer to the entire course and any additional material when used in reference an online or 'computer formatted' classroom. Many companies are using the term to describe the entire "package" consisting of one 'class' or 'course' bundled together with the various lessons, tests, and other material needed. The courseware itself can be in different formats, some are only available online such as html pages, while others can be downloaded in pdf files or other types of document files. Many forms of e-learning are now being blended with term courseware. Most leading educational companies solicit or include courseware with their training packages. In 1992 a company called SCORE! Educational Centers formed to deliver to individual consumers courseware based on personalization technology that was previously only available to select schools and the Education Programme for Gifted Youth.

Classroom Aids

A further category of educational software is software designed for use in school classrooms. Typically such software may be projected onto a large whiteboard at the front of the class and/or run simultaneously on a network of desktop computers in a classroom. This type of software is often called classroom management software. While teachers often choose to use educational software from other categories in their IT suites (e.g. reference works, children's software), a whole category of educational software has grown up specifically intended to assist classroom teaching. Branding has been less strong in this category than in those categories orientated towards home users. Software titles are often very specialised and produced by a wide variety of manufacturers, including many established educational book publishers.

- *The schoolzone.co.uk Guide to Digital Resources, 5th ed. (2005)* - An up-to-date full-colour guide with reviews of around 500 selected and recommended products, categorised by subject area, albeit specific to the UK school system.

Edutainment

In a broader sense, the term *edutainment* describes an intentional merger of computer games and educational software into a single product (and could therefore also comprise more serious titles described above under children's learning software). In the narrower sense used here, the term describes educational software which is primarily about entertainment, but tends to educate as well and sells itself partly under the educational umbrella. Software of this kind is not structured towards school curricula, does not normally involve educational advisors, and does not focus on core skills such as literacy and numeracy.

Reference Software

Many publishers of print dictionaries and encyclopedias have been involved in the production of educational reference software since the mid-1990s. They were joined in the reference software market by both startup companies and established software publishers, most notably Microsoft.

The first commercial reference software products were reformulations of existing content into CD-ROM editions, often supplemented with new multimedia content, including compressed video and sound. More recent products made use of internet technologies, to supplement CD-ROM products, then, more recently, to replace them entirely.

Previously, encyclopedias and dictionaries had compiled their contents on the basis of invited and closed teams of specialists. The Wiki concept has allowed for the development of collaborative reference works through open cooperation incorporating experts and non-experts.

Educational Software on Custom Platforms

Some manufacturers regarded normal desktop computers as an inappropriate platform for learning software for younger children and produced custom child-friendly pieces of hardware instead. The hardware and software is generally combined into a single product, such as a child-sized laptop-lookalike. The most well-known example are Leapfrog products.

These include imaginatively designed hand-held consoles with a variety of pluggable educational game cartridges and book-like electronic devices into which a variety of electronic books can be loaded.

These products are more portable than laptop computers, but have a much more limited range of purposes, concentrating on literacy and numeracy.

Computer Games with Learning Value

These are games which were originally developed for adults or older children and which have potential learning implications. For the most part, these games provide simulations of different kinds of human activities, allowing players to explore a variety of social, historical and economic processes.

For example:

- City-building games such as the SimCity series (1989-2003) and Caesar (video game) (1993-2006) invite players to explore the social, practical and economic processes involved in city management;

- Empire-building games such as the Civilization (video game) series (1991-2005) and the Europa Universalis series (2000-2007) help players to learn about history and its political, economic and military aspects;
- Railroad management games such as Railroad Tycoon (1990-2003) and Rails Across America (2001) illuminate the history, engineering and economics of railroad management.

Do games such as these qualify as edutainment? To do so, they would need to have been created with a clear educational intent. In their publicity material, the developers of these games such as these generally focus more on the 'fun' aspects of the games rather than their educational potential. This might be taken as evidence of an absence of educational intent. On the other hand, large amounts of information of an overtly educational nature may be found within the manuals of many of these games, suggesting that education was indeed very much in the minds of the developers. Accordingly, these games may be classified as edutainment.

In any event, the games have been enthusiastically received in some educational circles and even passed into academic literature.

Software in Corporate Training and Tertiary Education

Earlier educational software for the important corporate and tertiary education markets was designed to run on a single desktop computer (or an equivalent user device). The history of such software is usefully summarized in the *SCORM 2004 2nd edition Overview* (section 1.3), unfortunately, however, without precise dates. In the years immediately following 2000, planners decided to switch to server-based applications with a high degree of standardization. This means that educational software runs primarily on servers which may be hundreds or thousands of miles from the actual user. The user only receives tiny pieces of a learning module or test, fed over the internet one by one. The server software decides on what learning material to distribute, collects results and displays progress to teaching staff. Another way of expressing this change is to say that educational software morphed into an online educational service. US Governmental endorsements and approval systems ensured the rapid switch to the new way of managing and distributing learning material.

Software for Specific Educational Purposes

There are highly specific niche markets for educational software, including:

- Language learning software (Kverbos or English in a Flash, for example)
- Typing tutors (Mario Teaches Typing or Mavis Beacon, for example)
- Driving test software
- Software for enabling simulated dissection of human and animal bodies (used in medical and veterinary college courses)
- Interactive geometry software
- Medical and healthcare educational software
- Spelling tutor software.

11
Computer and Digital Technology

A Computer-Based Assessment (CBA), also known as Computer-Based Testing (CBT), e-exam, computerized testing and computer-administered testing, is a method of administering tests in which the responses are electronically recorded, assessed, or both. As the name implies, Computer-Based Assessment makes use of a computer or an equivalent electronic device (i.e. handheld computer). CBA systems enables educators and trainers to author, schedule, deliver, and report on surveys, quizzes, tests and exams.

Computer-Based Assessment may be a stand-alone system or a part of a virtual learning environment, possibly accessed via the World Wide Web.

General advantages of Computer-Based Assessment (CBA) systems over traditional Pen-and-Paper Testing (PPT) have been demonstrated in several comparative works and includes: increased delivery, administration and scoring efficiency; reduced costs for many elements of the testing lifecycle; improved test security resulting from electronic transmission and encryption; consistency and reliability; faster and more controlled test revision process with shorter response time; faster decision-making as the result of immediate scoring and reporting; unbiased test administration and scoring; fewer response entry and recognition errors; fewer comprehension errors caused by the testing process; improved translation and localization with universal availability of content; new advanced and flexible item types; increased candidate acceptance and satisfaction; evolutionary step toward future testing methodologies.

In addition to traditional testing approaches carried out in a paper-pencil mode, there are a variety of aspects needed to be taken into account when computer-based assessment (CBA) is deployed, such as software quality, secure delivery, reliable network (if Internet-based), capacities, support, maintenance, software costs for development and test delivery, including licences. Any of the delivery modes, whether Paper-Pencil and/or computer-based, comprises advantages and challenges which can hardly be compared, especially in relation to estimated costs. The use of CBA includes additional benefits which can be achieved from an organisational, psychological, analytical and pedagogical perspective. Many experts agree on the overall added value and advantages of e-testing in large scale assessments.

It is also envisaged that computer-based formative assessment, in particular, will play an increasingly important role in learning, with the increased use of banks of question items for the construction and delivery of dynamic, on-demand assessments. This can be witnessed by current pioneering projects such as the SQA's SOLAR Project.

COMPUTERIZED ADAPTIVE TESTING

Computerized adaptive testing (**CAT**) is a form of computer-based test that adapts to the examinee's ability level. For this reason, it has also been called *tailored testing*.

How CAT Works

CAT successively selects questions so as to maximize the precision of the exam based on what is known about the examinee from previous questions. From the examinee's perspective, the difficulty of the exam seems to tailor itself to his or her level of ability. For example, if an examinee performs well on an item of intermediate difficulty, he will then be presented with a more difficult question. Or, if he performed poorly, he would be presented with a simpler question. Compared to static multiple choice tests that nearly everyone has experienced, with a fixed set of items administered to all examinees, computer-adaptive tests require fewer test items to arrive at equally accurate scores. (Of course, there is nothing about the CAT methodology that requires the items to be multiple-choice; but just as most exams are multiple-choice, most CAT exams also use this format.)

The basic computer-adaptive testing method is an iterative algorithm with the following steps:

1. The pool of available items is searched for the optimal item, based on the current estimate of the examinee's ability.

2. The chosen item is presented to the examinee, who then answers it correctly or incorrectly.

3. The ability estimate is updated, based upon all prior answers.

4. Steps 1–3 are repeated until a termination criterion is met.

Nothing is known about the examinee prior to the administration of the first item, so the algorithm is generally started by selecting an item of medium, or medium-easy, difficulty as the first item.

As a result of adaptive administration, different examinees receive quite different tests. The psychometric technology that allows equitable scores to be computed across different sets of items is item response theory (IRT). IRT is also the preferred methodology for selecting optimal items which are typically selected on the basis of *information* rather than difficulty, per se.

The GRE General Test and the Graduate Management Admission Test are currently primarily administered as a computer-adaptive test. A list of active CAT programs is found at CAT Central, along with a list of current CAT research programs and a near-inclusive bibliography of all published CAT research.

A related methodology called multistage testing (MST) or CAST is used in the Uniform Certified Public Accountant Examination. MST avoids or reduces some of the disadvantages of CAT as described below.

Advantages

Adaptive tests can provide uniformly precise scores for most test-takers. In contrast, standard fixed tests almost always provide the best precision for test-takers of medium ability and increasingly poorer precision for test-takers with more extreme test scores.

An adaptive test can typically be shortened by 50% and still maintain a higher level of precision than a fixed version. This translates into a time savings for the test-taker. Test-takers do not waste their time attempting items that are too hard or trivially easy. Additionally, the testing organization benefits from the time savings; the cost of examinee seat time is substantially reduced. However, because the development of a CAT involves much more expense than a standard fixed-form test, a large population is necessary for a CAT testing program to be financially fruitful.

Like any computer-based test, adaptive tests may show results immediately after testing.

Adaptive testing, depending on the item selection algorithm, may reduce exposure of some items because examinees typically receive different sets of items rather than the whole population being administered a single set. However, it may increase the exposure of others (namely the medium or medium/easy items presented to most examinees at the beginning of the test).

Disadvantages

The first issue encountered in CAT is the calibration of the item pool. In order to model the characteristics of the items (e.g., to pick the optimal item), all the items of the test must be pre-administered to a sizable sample and then analyzed. To achieve this, new items must be mixed into the operational items of an exam (the responses are recorded but do not contribute to the test-takers' scores), called "pilot testing," "pre-testing," or "seeding." This presents logistical, ethical, and security issues. For example, it is impossible to field an operational adaptive test with brand-new, unseen items; all items must be pretested with a large enough sample to obtain stable item statistics. This sample may be required to be as large as 1,000 examinees. Each program must decide what percentage of the test can reasonably be composed of unscored pilot test items.

Although adaptive tests have *exposure control* algorithms to prevent overuse of a few items, the exposure conditioned upon ability is often not controlled and can easily become close to 1. That is, it is common for some items to become very common on tests for people of the same ability. This is a serious security concern because groups sharing items may well have a similar functional ability level. In fact, a completely randomized exam is the most secure (but also least efficient).

Review of past items is generally disallowed. Adaptive tests tend to administer easier items after a person answers incorrectly. Supposedly, an astute test-taker could use such clues to detect incorrect answers and correct them. Or, test-takers could be coached to deliberately pick wrong answers, leading to an increasingly easier test. After tricking the adaptive test into building a maximally easy exam, they could then review the items and answer them correctly—possibly achieving a very high score. Test-takers frequently complain about the inability to review.

CAT Components

There are five technical components in building a CAT (the following is adapted from Weiss & Kingsbury, 1984). This list does not include practical issues, such as item pretesting or live field release.

1. Calibrated item pool
2. Starting point or entry level
3. Item selection algorithm
4. Scoring procedure
5. Termination criterion

Calibrated Item Pool

A pool of items must be available for the CAT to choose from. The pool must be calibrated with a psychometric model, which is used as a basis for the remaining four components. Typically, item response theory is employed as the psychometric model. One reason item response theory is popular is because it places persons and items on the same metric (denoted by the Greek letter theta), which is helpful for issues in item selection.

Starting Point

In CAT, items are selected based on the examinee's performance up to a given point in the test. However, the CAT is obviously not able to make any specific estimate of examinee ability when no items have been administered. So some other initial estimate of examinee ability is necessary. If some previous information regarding the examinee is known, it can be used, but often the CAT just assumes that the examinee is of average ability - hence the first item often being of medium difficulty.

Item Selection Algorithm

As mentioned previously, item response theory places examinees and items on the same metric. Therefore, if the CAT has an estimate of examinee ability, it is able to select an item that is most appropriate for that estimate. Technically, this is done by selecting the item with the greatest *information* at that point. Information is a function of the discrimination parameter of the item, as well as the conditional variance and pseudoguessing parameter (if used).

Scoring Procedure

After an item is administered, the CAT updates its estimate of the examinee's ability level. If the examinee answered the item correctly, the CAT will likely estimate their ability to be somewhat higher, and vice versa. This is done by using the item response function from item response theory to obtain a likelihood function of the examinee's ability. Two methods for this are called *maximum likelihood estimation* and *Bayesian estimation*. The latter assumes an *a priori* distribution of examinee ability, and has two commonly used estimators: *expectation a posteriori* and *maximum a posteriori*. Maximum likelihood is equivalent to a Bayes maximum a posterior estimate if a uniform (f(x)=1) prior is assumed. Maximum likelihood is asymptotically unbiased, but cannot provide a theta estimate for a nonmixed (all correct or incorrect) response vector, in which case a Bayesian method may have to be used temporarily.

Termination Criterion

The CAT algorithm is designed to repeatedly administer items and update the estimate of examinee ability. This will continue until the item pool is exhausted unless a termination criterion is incorporated into the CAT. Often, the test is terminated when the examinee's standard error of measurement falls below a certain user-specified value, hence, the statement above that an advantage is that examinee scores will be uniformly precise or "equiprecise." Other termination criteria exist for different purposes of the test, such as if the test is designed only to determine if the examinee is should "Pass" or "Fail" the test, rather than obtaining a precise estimate of their ability.

Other Issues

Pass-Fail CAT

In many situations, the purpose of the test is to classify examinees into two or more mutually exclusive and exhaustive categories. This includes the common "mastery test" where the two classifications are "pass" and "fail," but also includes situations where there are three or more classifications, such as "Insufficient," "Basic," and "Advanced" levels of knowledge or competency. The kind of "item-level adaptive" CAT described in this article is most appropriate for tests that are not "pass/fail" or for pass/fail tests where providing good feedback is extremely important.) Some modifications are necessary for a pass/fail CAT, also known as a computerized classification test (CCT). For examinees with true scores very close to the passing score, computerized classification tests will result in long tests while those with true scores far above or below the passing score will have shortest exams.

For example, a new termination criterion and scoring algorithm must be applied that classifies the examinee into a category rather than providing a point estimate of ability. There are two primary methodologies available for this. The more prominent of the two is the sequential probability ratio test (SPRT). This formulates the examinee classification problem as a hypothesis test that the examinee's ability is equal to either some specified point above the cutscore or another specified point below the cutscore. Note that this is a point hypothesis formulation rather than a composite hypothesis formulation that is more conceptually appropriate. A composite hypothesis formulation would be that the examinee's ability is in the region above the cutscore or the region below the cutscore.

A confidence interval approach is also used, where after each item is administered, the algorithm determines the probability that the examinee's true-score is above or below the passing score. For example, the algorithm may continue until the 95% confidence interval for the true score no longer contains the passing score. At that point, no further items are needed because the pass-fail decision is already 95% accurate, assuming that the psychometric models underlying the adaptive testing fit the examinee and test. This approach was originally called "adaptive mastery testing" but it can be applied to non-adaptive item selection and classification situations of two or more cutscores.

As a practical matter, the algorithm is generally programmed to have a minimum and a maximum test length. Otherwise, it would be possible for an examinee with ability very close to the cutscore to be administered every item in the bank without the algorithm making a decision.

The item selection algorithm utilized depends on the termination criterion. Maximizing information at the cutscore is more appropriate for the SPRT because it maximizes the difference in the probabilities used in the likelihood ratio. Maximizing information at the ability estimate is more appropriate for the confidence interval approach because it minimizes the conditional standard error of measurement, which decreases the width of the confidence interval needed to make a classification.

Practical Constraints of Adaptivity

ETS researcher Martha Stocking has quipped that most adaptive tests are actually *barely adaptive tests* (BATs) because, in practice, many constraints are imposed upon item choice. For example, CAT exams must usually meet content specifications; a verbal exam may need to be composed of equal numbers of analogies, fill-in-the-blank and synonym item types. CATs typically have some form of item exposure constraints, to prevent the most informative items from being over-exposed. Also, on some tests, an attempt is made to balance surface characteristics of the items such as gender of the people in the items or the ethnicities implied by their names. Thus CAT exams are frequently constrained in which items it may choose and for some exams the constraints may be substantial and require complex search strategies (e.g., linear programming) to find suitable items.

Computerized Classification Test

A **computerized classification test** (CCT) refers to, as its name would suggest, a test that is administered by computer for the purpose of classifying examinees. The most common CCT is a mastery test where the test classifies examinees as "Pass" or "Fail," but the term also includes tests that classify examinees into more than two categories. While the term may generally be considered to refer to all computer-administered tests for classification, it is usually used to refer to tests that are interactively administered or of variable-length, similar to computerized adaptive testing (CAT). Like CAT, variable-length CCTs can accomplish the goal of the test (accurate classification) with a fraction of the number of items used in a conventional fixed-form test.

A CCT requires several components:

1. An item bank calibrated with a psychometric model selected by the test designer
2. A starting point
3. An item selection algorithm
4. A termination criterion and scoring procedure

The starting point is not a topic of contention; research on CCT primarily investigates the application of different methods for the other three components. *Note:* The termination criterion and scoring procedure are separate in CAT, but the same in CCT because the test is terminated when a classification is made. Therefore, there are five components that must be specified to design a CAT.

An introduction to CCT is found in Thompson (2007) and a book by Parshall, Spray, Kalohn and Davey (2006). A bibliography of published CCT research is found below.

How a CCT Works?

A CCT is very similar to a CAT. Items are administered one at a time to an examinee. After the examinee responds to the item, the computer scores it and determines if the examinee is able to be classified yet. If they are, the test is terminated and the examinee is classified. If not, another item is administered. This process repeats until the examinee is classified or another ending point is satisfied (all items in the bank have been administered, or a maximum test length is reached).

Psychometric Model

Two approaches are available for the psychometric model of a CCT: classical test theory (CTT) and item response theory (IRT). Classical test theory assumes a state model because it is applied by determining item parameters for a sample of examinees determined to be in each category. For instance, several hundred "masters" and several hundred "nonmasters" might be sampled to determine the difficulty and discrimination for each, but doing so requires that you be able to easily identify a distinct set of people that are in each group. IRT, on the other hand, assumes a trait model; the knowledge or ability measured by the test is a continuum. The classification groups will need to be more or less arbitrarily defined along the continuum, such as the use of a cutscore to demarcate masters and nonmasters, but the specification of item parameters assumes a trait model.

There are advantages and disadvantages to each. CTT offers greater conceptual simplicity. More importantly, CTT requires fewer examinees in the sample for calibration of item parameters to be used eventually in the design of the CCT, making it useful for smaller testing programmes. See Frick (1992) for a description of a CTT-based CCT. Most CCTs, however, utilize IRT. IRT offers greater specificity, but the most important reason may be that the design of a CCT (and a CAT) is expensive, and is therefore more likely done by a large testing programme with extensive resources. Such a programme would likely use IRT.

Starting Point

A CCT must have a specified starting point to enable certain algorithms. If the sequential probability ratio test is used as the termination criterion, it implicitly assumes a starting ratio of 1.0 (equal probability of the examinee being a master or nonmaster). If the termination criterion is a confidence interval approach, a specified starting point on theta must be specified. Usually, this is 0.0, the centre of the distribution, but it could also be randomly drawn from a certain distribution if the parameters of the examinee distribution are known. Also, previous information regarding an individual examinee, such as their score the last time they took the test (if re-taking) may be used.

Item Selection

In a CCT, items are selected for administration throughout the test, unlike the traditional method of administering a fixed set of items to all examinees. While this is usually done by individual item, it can also be done in groups of items known as testlets.

Methods of item selection fall into two categories: cutscore-based and estimate-based. Cutscore-based methods (also known as sequential selection) maximize the information provided by the item at the cutscore, or cutscores if there are more than one, regardless of the ability of the examinee. Estimate-based methods (also known as adaptive selection) maximize information at the current estimate of examinee ability, regardless of the location of the cutscore. Both work efficiently, but the efficiency depends in part on the termination criterion employed. Because the sequential probability ratio test only evaluates probabilities near the cutscore, cutscore-based item selection is more appropriate. Because the confidence interval termination criterion is centered around the examinees ability estimate, estimate-based item selection is more appropriate. This is because the test will make a classification when the confidence interval is small enough to be completely above or below the cutscore. The confidence interval will be smaller when the standard error of measurement is smaller, and the standard error of measurement will be smaller when there is more information at the theta level of the examinee.

Termination Criterion

There are three termination criteria commonly used for CCTs. Bayesian decision theory methods offer great flexibility by presenting an infinite choice of loss/utility structures and evaluation considerations, but also introduce greater arbitrariness. A confidence interval approach calculates a confidence interval around the examinee's current theta estimate at each point in the test, and classifies the examinee when the interval falls completely within a region of theta that defines a classification. This was originally known as adaptive mastery testing, but does not necessarily require adaptive item selection, nor is it limited to the two-classification mastery testing situation. The sequential probability ratio test defines the classification problem as a hypothesis test that the examinee's theta is equal to a specified point above the cutscore or a specified point below the cutscore.

DIVO Project

DIVO (Digital Interactive Video Online), is an active learning education concept, incorporating creativity and ICTs, which uses participant centred, creative digital video dialogue(s) to promote inter-cultural understanding and peer-led learning between remote groups who would otherwise never be able to meet.

The DIVO project uses digital video to enrich online dialogue between remote groups. Groups of young people conceive, record and exchange short digital films based on common themes which are shared via a website. The films are viewed and the issues contained are discussed and explored on and offline and new films are created and shared in response. In this way, a digital video dialogue emerges which contains a genuine sense of mutual sharing and exchange. DIVO can be used in a range of settings to promote and support dialogue in formal and informal educational contexts, including inter-cultural understanding in support of Key Stages 3 and 4. Learning how to use digital interactive video creatively is coupled with the development of teamwork and negotiation skills. Mass media often promotes images and messages which are at odds with the environment and unrelated to the audience. The DIVO project puts media creation firmly in the hands of participants, offering them the opportunity to experiment in a playful and powerful way with a media force they are only likely to have experienced as consumers.

The DIVO project is committed to relocating remote and marginalised groups to the centre of the communication process and giving their voices a global platform.

In 2004, the DIVO project successfully bought together two groups of girls: socially and economically marginalised young women from an Islamic community in Ghana and students from Elizabeth Garrett Anderson School for Girls in London, UK. The project facilitated a cultural exchange based on gender issues faced by participants in the groups. By creating and responding to each others' films, participants enjoyed a rich experience of reflection and analysis. Dialogues formed through the process have continued to develop beyond the initial life of the pilot project. The pilot phase was funded by the British Council, the British High Commission and the Guardian Newspaper Ltd.

A full evaluative report and 20-min project documentary are available. The project documentary has been recognised by selection in a number of international human rights film festivals and screens regularly on the Community Channel in the UK.

Methodology

The methodology of DIVO comes from the combination of the creative application of technology with peer-led, participant-centred teaching techniques. As emphasis is as strongly placed on the process of generating media clips as on the media clips themselves, DIVO offers a rich multi-strand learning opportunity. The activity that goes into creating a media product for an audience of peers is both an opportunity and motivation for learning. In order to create a dialogue, groups need to digest what they have viewed and examine this against their existing knowledge before proceeding to generate more media and develop their response. Because media generated is personally relevant and specifically created, it is more compelling for participants to engage with and reflect on. DIVO can operate as a multi-lateral dialogue between many groups and offers flexibility of access to audiences and freedom of timing.

Desire2Learn

Desire2Learn Incorporated ("D2L") is a global provider of enterprise eLearning solutions and develops online Learning Management Systems (LMS) for schools, higher education, associations, government and private industry. Today the company and its subsidiaries support more than 5 million learners worldwide. In 2008, Desire2Learn was ranked, for the third consecutive year, amongst the fastest growing technology companies in Canada by the Deloitte Technology Fast 50 program. Revenue growth of 920% from Jan 1, 2003 to Dec 31, 2007 resulted in the 23rd place ranking for Desire2Learn, which is an organically-grown and self-funded company. Founded in April 1999, by President and CEO John Baker, the company is headquartered in Kitchener, Ontario, Canada, and has personnel located in the U.S., Canada, the U.K. and Australia.

eLearning Enterprise Suite

The Enterprise eLearning suite provided by Desire2Learn includes:

- **Learning Environment** – a web-based suite of teaching and learning tools that provide course development, delivery and management.
- **ePortfolio** – a system for collecting, organizing, reflecting on, and presenting learning artifacts. It can be used for presenting materials for assignments, working on group projects, peer review, resume creation and job seeking, and developing a full electronic portfolio of work. It can also be used for social learning applications.
- **Competencies** – a comprehensive and flexible suite of Competency tracking and reporting tools.
- **Analytics** – a business intelligence solution which provides transparency to all of the various datasets that make up the Desire2Learn Learning Environment.

- **Learning Repository** — an integrated standards-based Learning Object Repository that provides storing, tagging, researching and reusing of learning objects.
- **LiveRoom** — a set of communication tools to enable real-time collaboration between instructors and students.
- **Essentials** — a smaller set of web-based tools that provide course development, delivery and management.
- **Desire2Learn 2GO** — a mobile learning application that lets users access course information from a BlackBerry mobile device.

Technology Partners

The company has established partnerships with Aventa Learning, Inc.; Cengage Learning; Elluminate; IBM; iParadigms, LLC; McGraw Hill Education; Microsoft; Respondus; Sun Microsystems; SunGard Higher Education; Pearson Education Inc. and The Learning Edge International Pty Ltd.

Legal Issues

According to Desire2Learn's PatentInfo Blog, Desire2Learn won their Appeal in the Federal Circuit — the judgment was reversed and the claims asserted are now invalid. Desire2Learn and Blackboard have also settled their other litigation.,

Destiny Solutions

Destiny Solutions is a North American provider of administrative software for continuing education. Founded in 2001 by president and CEO, Shaul Kuper, Destiny Solutions is based in Toronto, Ontario, Canada. Destiny's clients include many high-profile organizations across Canada and the US.

Destiny OneCE

This enterprise software suite includes:

- **Views**—Personalized portals into the data customized to four roles (Public, Student, Staff, Instructor)
- **Modules**
  - o Registration
  - o Curriculum
  - o Marketing
  - o Finance
- **Extensions**—integration with:
  - o Student Information Systems: PeopleSoft Campus Solutions, Banner, Datatel
  - o Financial Systems: Oracle, SAP, Great Plains, Banner
  - o CRM systems: Salesforce.com, Intelliworks, Talisma, Constant Contact
  - o Learning management: Blackboard, Sakai, Moodle, Desire2Learn
  - o Authentication systems: CAS, Shibboleth, Tivoli, LDAP, Active Directory
- **Destiny I-Services**—A set of services and plug-ins for integration with main campus systems

Digital Audio Learning Objects

The **Digital Audio Learning Object** (DALO) concept was devised at Sheffield Hallam University in the UK as a simple design methodology for non-technical staff and students. The concept embodies reusable learning object theory alongside theory pertaining to the effective and creative use of digital audio to enhance learning.

A DALO is a digital audio file, designed collaboratively by students or academic staff through a process facilitated by design tools. As with other learning objects, the DALO can be used, and reused, in various learning situations. The design process offers a Communal Constructivist and Constructionist learning opportunity in the first instance, with the resulting product then becoming a valuable resource for fellow learners.

The finished DALOs are intended to be used as short 'media interventions' that lead into other learning activity. They are not intended to transmit substantial learning content, being more associated more with active learning philosophies.

Tools to facilitate a creative design process, especially where media design is not central to practice, have been devised. These include a design specification proforma and an associated taxonomy of professional voices.

Key Concepts

Simple to use

A single, easy to produce and manage audio file in a common format (MP3).

Simple to Produce

The DALO has a well-defined and limited scope. This ensures that these useful resources can be easily designed and produced with little technical knowledge. Ambitious ideas, such as well developed 'programmes', are not likely to be DALOs because their increased sophistication will undoubtedly limit reusability and depend upon technical expertise in their production and distribution.

Immediate

DALOs are cheap to make and can be available quickly. Imagine one or two people speaking into a tape recorder and this recording being available from Blackboard within minutes for students to take away. This is what is possible.

Educationally Focussed

Designing to support a distinct learning objective ensures that the DALO will satisfy its original, primary purpose. Reusability of learning content is desirable for economic reasons as long as educational integrity is not undermined.

However, DALOs may have a purpose beyond the original intention. For example, it may become useful in another subject area, with another cohort, or to reinforce understanding at a later stage.

Reusable

'The voice of the teacher' (also known as interpretation or mediation) happens outside of the DALO in the VLE, the lecture theatre or elsewhere. This means the DALO can be interpreted according to the needs of any learning context. In this way a particular DALO could be used in introducing an idea and again in an assessment, for example.

Engaging

It is difficult to keep an audience's attention for prolonged periods of time by audio alone. Also we need to accept that we are not professional actors and script writers.

Therefore that digital audio is best used selectively to capture attention, to deliver points succinctly (e.g. to summarise) and to illustrate and 'add colour' to the learning experience.

Digital Storytelling

Digital Storytelling refers to using digital tools so that ordinary people can tell their own real-life stories.

An Emerging Term

"Digital Storytelling" is an emerging term, one that arises from a grassroots movement that uses new digital tools to help ordinary people tell their own 'true stories' in a compelling and emotionally engaging form. These stories usually take the form of a relatively short story (less than 8 minutes) and can involve interactivity.

The term can also be a broader journalistic reference to the variety of emergent new forms of digital narratives (web-based stories, interactive stories, hypertexts, and narrative computer games).

As an emerging area of creative work, the definition of digital storytelling is still the subject of much debate.

Development and Pioneers

The broad definition has been used by innumerable artists and producers to link their practices with traditions of oral storytelling and often to delineate work from the highly produced commercial or conceptual projects by focusing on authorship and humanistic or emotionally provocative content. Some of the artists that have self-described as digital storytellers included Joe Lambert, Abbe Don, Brenda Laurel, Dana Atchley, and Pedro Meyer.

The short narrated films definition of digital storytelling relates back to the development of a production workshop by Dana Atchley at the American Film Institute in 1993 that was adapted and refined by Joe Lambert in the mid-1990's into a method of training promoted by the San Francisco Bay Area-based Center for Digital Storytelling.

Typically, digital stories are produced in intensive workshops. The product is a 2-5 minute film that combines a narrated piece of personal writing, photographic and other still images, and a musical soundtrack. The philosophy behind this type of digital storytelling is using technology to enable those without a technical background to produce works that tell a story using "moving" images and sound. The lower machine requirements for using stills rather than video, and the ease of use of iMovie with the so-called "Ken Burns" pan effect, allowed for the creation of short films by non-techies.

Digital storytelling is evolving from the simple narrated video to forms with interactivity and higher production values. These include websites and online videos created to promote causes, entertain, educate, and inform audiences.

Use by Public Broadcasters and Education

This model has been integrated into public broadcasting by the BBC'sCapture Wales project. The following year a similar project was launched by the BBC in England called Telling Lives. Swedish Educational Media company UR created Room for Storytelling, Netherlands Educational TV Tealac-NOT created a programme with youth in Amsterdam. KQED, Rocky Mountain PBS, WETA and other public television stations in the US have developed projects.

The Center for Digital Storytelling model has also been adopted in education, especially in the US, where some practitioners use it as a method of building engagement and multimedia literacy. For example, the Bay Area Video Coalition employs digital storytelling as a means of engaging and empowering at-risk youth.

Uses in Primary and Secondary Education: Faculty and graduate students at the University of Houston have created a website called the Educational Uses of Digital Storytelling which focuses on the use of Digital Storytelling by teachers and their students across multiple content areas and grade levels.

The National Writing Project (NWP) has a collaboration with the Pearson Foundation examining the literacy practices involved in their [[digital storytelling]] work with students.

Uses in Higher Education: The distribution of Digital Storytelling in Higher Education emerged in the late nineties with the Center for Digital Storytelling collaborating with a number of Universities while based at UC Berkeley. CDS programs with the New Media Consortium led to links to many campuses, where ongoing programs in Digital Storytelling have grown including Cal State Monterey, Ohio State University, Williams College, MIT, University of Maryland Baltimore, County, and the University of Wisconsin, Madison and dozens of others. In addition, Kean University, Virginia Tech, Simmons College, Swarthmore College, University of Colorado, Denver, the University of Calgary, University of Massachusetts (Amherst), and others have developed ongoing programs.

Starting in 2001, Rina Benmayor (from California State University-Monterey Bay) hosted a Center for Digital Storytelling seminar on her campus and began using digital storytelling in her latino/a life stories classes. Benmayor began sharing that work with faculty across the country including Georgetown University; LaGuardia Community College, CUNY; Millersville University; Vanderbilt University, and University of Wisconsin–Stout.

Uses in Public Health, Social Services, and International Development: The development of the Silence Speaks project in 1999 under the direction Amy Hill (who joined the Center for Digital Storytelling in 2005) led to the expansion of Digital Storytelling in countless contexts of public health. Projects developed with the Center for Disease Control, the Open Society Foundation, work in Gender-based violence prevention with groups in California, Texas, New York, Minnesota, and with the organization Sonke Gender Justice in South Africa, the broad use of Digital Storytelling with Foster Youth, and finally the connection to Digital Storytelling to public campaigns in substance abuse prevention and community mental health programmes.

Uses in Museums: Digital storytelling is being used by many different museums, the largest scale project being the work of the Australian Center for the Moving Image. The National Gallery of Art in Washington D.C. also held a series of trainings to integrate arts education curriculum with Digital Storytelling from 2003-2005. Some museums to help interpret and make community history accessible. In 2007, the Colorado Historical Society collaborated with the Center for Digital Storytelling to create a programme, the Italians about Italian American History. In 2008, a group of eleven museums in Yorkshire launched My Yorkshire ; a digital storytelling project. The museums work with communities to use contemporary collected oral histories alongside those from archives to interpret local history from a personal point of view. Some interesting issues have arisen with the use of historical oral recordings and archival photos. The group have also produced help guides to creating digital stories in a museum setting. The finished digital stories can have many uses from advertising an upcoming exhibition or being a lasting legacy of a short term project to building relations with communiities, 'up-skilling' volunteers and being displayed as permanent features in galleries.

Place-based Digital Storytelling

The Canadian Film Centre's New Media Lab (formerly MediaLinx Habitat)launched a project Murmur out of the 2002-2003 studio. The project integrates audio interviews into cell phone based tours. The Center for Digital Storytelling created Storymapping.org in 2006 with projects in Mendocino, Ca, Houston, Texas, New Orleans, Tuscaloosa, Alabama to promote the connection between storytelling and issues of local memory and civic planning.

Digital Technologies in Education

Digital technology is a term that is being increasingly used in education in place of the now dated terms like ICT, educational technology, computer based education and technology enhanced learning.

The term digital technologies is used to refer to the ever-evolving suite of digital software, hardware and architecture used in learning and teaching in the school, the home and beyond the home and school environments.

It is used in such diverse recent education writings from across the world as Prensky (2007), Schools in the Digital Age (2007), Media and Communications in Australian Families 2007 (2007), Lee and Gaffney (2008), Lee and Winzenried (2009) and Davidson and Goldberg (2009). It is used particularly in preference to the term 'ICT' which is seen as not only being limited, lacking precision and being dated but most importantly the acronym ICT does not adequately communicate the full implications of being digital, with its facility for increasing convergence and integration, and its impact upon traditionally discrete operations.

By referring to digital technologies, one accommodates the evolution of a suite of integrated digital technologies that can be accessed virtually anywhere, anytime. They are far more than just a few discrete technologies. Rather, it is about the use and impact of an ever-evolving suite of increasingly integrated digital technologies conceptualized as part of a digital ecosystem that can be adapted, based on needs and context. To illustrate, the smart phone, viewed as a digital technology, rather than a discrete technology, can be used as a phone, a camera, an MP3 player, or computer, or any blended combination of those functionalities, and in seamless conjunction with other digital technologies. In this way, digital technologies become defined in terms of the user's need and context, shaping the ways in which the digital applications are used in multiple ways and with multiple digital applications.

The concept of digital technologies also addresses the reality that the young enhance their learning informally, by teaching themselves how to use and apply the technologies and formally under guidance of teachers. However the other reality is that the youth of the developed world use the suite of digital technologies far more outside the formal teaching situation than within and that formal classroom use constitutes only a minor part of the total overall use. Little is the surprise, as Meredyth *et al* and others have identified, the young acquire their digital competencies more outside the classroom than within.

In using the term 'digital technologies' one is also recognising that the young have these in their homes and on the move have normalised the use of an ever-evolving suite of digital technologies, use different elements of the suite in different situations and as such acquire their digital competencies from using a suite of technologies rather than a discrete technology.

The implications for teaching and learning – and indeed for the design of future curriculum — and for educational research are very considerable.

●●

12
Educational Assessment

Educational assessment is the process of documenting, usually in measurable terms, knowledge, skills, attitudes and beliefs. Assessment can focus on the individual learner, the learning community (class, workshop, or other organized group of learners), the institution, or the educational system as a whole. According to the Academic Exchange Quarterly:

> "Studies of a theoretical or empirical nature (including case studies, portfolio studies, exploratory, or experimental work) addressing the assessment of learner aptitude and preparation, motivation and learning styles, learning outcomes in achievement and satisfaction in different educational contexts are all welcome, as are studies addressing issues of measurable standards and benchmarks".

It is important to notice that the final purposes and assessment practices in education depends on the *theoretical framework* of the practitioners and researchers, their assumptions and beliefs about the nature of human mind, the origin of knowledge and the process of learning.

The following table summarizes the main *theoretical frameworks* behind almost all the theoretical and research work, and the instructional practices in education (one them being, of course, the practice of assessment).

This different frameworks have given rise to interesting debates among scholars.

Alternate Meanings

According to the Merriam-Webster online dictionary the word **assessment** comes from the root word *assess* which is defined as:

1. to determine the rate or amount of (as a tax)
2. to impose (as a tax) according to an established rate b: to subject to a tax, charge, or levy
3. to make an official valuation of (property) for the purposes of taxation
4. to determine the importance, size, or value of (assess a problem)
5. to charge (a player or team) with a foul or penalty

Assessment in education is best described as an action "to determine the importance, size, or value of."

Types

The term **assessment** is generally used to refer to all activities teachers use to help students learn and to gauge student progress. Though the notion of assessment is generally more complicated than the following categories suggest, assessment is often divided for the sake of convenience using the following distinctions:

1. Formative and summative
2. Objective and subjective
3. Referencing (criterion-referenced, norm-referenced, and ipsative)
4. Informal and formal.

Formative and Summative

Assessment is often divided into formative and summative categories for the purpose of considering different objectives for assessment practices.

- **Summative assessment** — Summative assessment is generally carried out at the end of a course or project. In an educational setting, summative assessments are typically used to assign students a course grade.
- **Formative assessment** — Formative assessment is generally carried out throughout a course or project. Formative assessment, also referred to as "educative assessment," is used to aid learning. In an educational setting, formative assessment might be a teacher (or peer) or the learner, providing feedback on a student's work, and would not necessarily be used for grading purposes.

Educational researcher Robert Stake explains the difference between formative and summative assessment with the following analogy:

> When the cook tastes the soup, that's formative. When the guests taste the soup, that's summative.

Summative and formative assessment are often referred to in a learning context as *assessment of learning* and *assessment for learning* respectively. Assessment of learning is generally summative in nature and intended to measure learning outcomes and report those outcomes to students, parents, and administrators. Assessment of learning generally occurs at the conclusion of a class, course, semester, or academic year. Assessment for learning is generally formative in nature and is used by teachers to consider approaches to teaching and next steps for individual learners and the class.

A common form of formative assessment is *diagnostic assessment*. Diagnostic assessment measures a student's current knowledge and skills for the purpose of identifying a suitable program of learning. *Self-assessment* is a form of diagnostic assessment which involves students assessing themselves. *Forward-looking assessment* asks those being assessed to consider themselves in hypothetical future situations.

Performance-based assessment is similar to summative assessment, as it focuses on achievement. It is often aligned with the standards-based education reform and outcomes-based education movement. Though ideally they are significantly different from a traditional multiple choice test, they are most commonly associated with standards-based assessment which use free-form responses to standard questions scored by human scorers on a standards-based scale, meeting, falling below, or exceeding a performance standard rather than being ranked on a curve. A well-defined task is identified and students are asked to create, produce, or do something, often in settings that involve real-world application of knowledge and skills. Proficiency is demonstrated by providing an extended response. Performance formats are further differentiated into products and performances. The performance may result in a product, such as a painting, portfolio, paper, or exhibition, or it may consist of a performance, such as a speech, athletic skill, musical recital, or reading.

Objective and Subjective

Assessment (either summative or formative) is often categorized as either objective or subjective. Objective assessment is a form of questioning which has a single correct answer. Subjective assessment is a form of questioning which may have more than one correct answer (or more than one way of expressing the correct answer). There are various types of objective and subjective questions. Objective question types include true/false answers, multiple choice, multiple-response and matching questions. Subjective questions include extended-response questions and essays. Objective assessment is well suited to the increasingly popular computerized or online assessment format.

Some have argued that the distinction between objective and subjective assessments is neither useful nor accurate because, in reality, there is no such thing as "objective" assessment. In fact, all assessments are created with inherent biases built into decisions about relevant subject matter and content, as well as cultural (class, ethnic, and gender) biases.

Basis of Comparison

Test results can be compared against an established criterion, or against the performance of other students, or against previous performance:

> *Criterion-referenced assessment,* typically using a criterion-referenced test, as the name implies, occurs when candidates are measured against defined (and objective) criteria. Criterion-referenced assessment is often, but not always, used to establish a person's competence (whether s/he can do something). The best known example of criterion-referenced assessment is the driving test, when learner drivers are measured against a range of explicit criteria (such as "Not endangering other road users").

Norm-referenced assessment (colloquially known as "grading on the curve"), typically using a norm-referenced test, is not measured against defined criteria. This type of assessment is relative to the student body undertaking the assessment. It is effectively a way of comparing students. The IQ test is the best known example of norm-referenced assessment. Many entrance tests (to prestigious schools or universities) are norm-referenced, permitting a fixed proportion of students to pass ("passing" in this context means being accepted into the school or university rather than an explicit level of ability). This means that standards may vary from year to year, depending on the quality of the cohort; criterion-referenced assessment does not vary from year to year (unless the criteria change).

Informal and Formal

Assessment can be either *formal* or *informal.* Formal assessment usually implicates a written document, such as a test, quiz, or paper. A formal assessment is given a numerical score or grade based on student performance, whereas an informal assessment does not contribute to a student's final grade. An informal assessment usually occurs in a more casual manner and may include observation, inventories, checklists, rating scales, rubrics, performance and portfolio assessments, participation, peer and self evaluation, and discussion.

Internal and External

Internal assessment is set and marked by the school (i.e. teachers). Students get the mark and feedback regarding the assessment. External assessment is set by the governing body, and is marked by non-biased personnel. With external assessment, students only receive a mark. Therefore, they have no idea how they actually performed (i.e. what bits they answered correctly.)

Standards of Quality

In general, high-quality assessments are considered those with a high level of reliability and validity. Approaches to reliability and validity vary, however.

Reliability

Reliability relates to the consistency of an assessment. A reliable assessment is one which consistently achieves the same results with the same (or similar) cohort of students. Various factors affect reliability – including ambiguous questions, too many options within a question paper, vague marking instructions and poorly trained markers. Traditionally, the reliability of an assessment is based on the following:

1. Temporal stability: Performance on a test is comparable on two or more separate occasions.
2. Form equivalence: Performance among examinees is equivalent on different forms of a test based on the same content.

3. Internal consistency: Responses on a test are consistent across questions. For example: In a survey that asks respondents to rate attitudes toward technology, consistency would be expected in responses to the following questions:
   - "I feel very negative about computers in general."
   - "I enjoy using computers."

Validity

A valid assessment is one which measures what it is intended to measure. For example, it would not be valid to assess driving skills through a written test alone. A more valid way of assessing driving skills would be through a combination of tests that help determine what a driver knows, such as through a written test of driving knowledge, and what a driver is able to do, such as through a performance assessment of actual driving. Teachers frequently complain that some examinations do not properly assess the syllabus upon which the examination is based; they are, effectively, questioning the validity of the exam.

Validity of an assessment is generally gauged through examination of evidence in the following categories:

1. **Content**—Does the content of the test measure stated objectives?
2. **Criterion**—Do scores correlate to an outside reference? (ex: Do high scores on a 4th grade reading test accurately predict reading skill in future grades?)
3. **Construct**—Does the assessment correspond to other significant variables? (ex: Do ESL students consistently perform differently on a writing exam than native English speakers?)

A good assessment has both validity and reliability, plus the other quality attributes noted above for a specific context and purpose. In practice, an assessment is rarely totally valid or totally reliable. A ruler which is marked wrong will always give the same (wrong) measurements. It is very reliable, but not very valid. Asking random individuals to tell the time without looking at a clock or watch is sometimes used as an example of an assessment which is valid, but not reliable. The answers will vary between individuals, but the average answer is probably close to the actual time. In many fields, such as medical research, educational testing, and psychology, there will often be a trade-off between reliability and validity. A history test written for high validity will have many essay and fill-in-the-blank questions. It will be a good measure of mastery of the subject, but difficult to score completely accurately. A history test written for high reliability will be entirely multiple choice. It isn't as good at measuring knowledge of history, but can easily be scored with great precision. We may generalise from this.

The more reliable is our estimate of what we purport to measure, the less certain we are that we are actually measuring that aspect of attainment. It is also important to note that there are at least thirteen sources of invalidity, which can be estimated for individual students in test situations. They never are. Perhaps this is because their social purpose demands the absence of any error, and validity errors are usually so high that they would destabilise the whole assessment industry.

It is well to distinguish between "subject-matter" validity and "predictive" validity. The former, used widely in education, predicts the score a student would get on a similar test but with different questions. The latter, used widely in the workplace, predicts performance. Thus, a subject-matter-valid test of knowledge of driving rules is appropriate while a predictively-valid test would assess whether the potential driver could follow those rules.

Testing Standards

In the field of psychometrics, the *Standards for Educational and Psychological Testing* place standards about validity and reliability, along with errors of measurement and related considerations under the general topic of test construction, evaluation and documentation. The second major topic covers standards related to fairness in testing, including fairness in testing and test use, the rights and responsibilities of test takers, testing individuals of diverse linguistic backgrounds, and testing individuals with disabilities. The third and final major topic covers standards related to testing applications, including the responsibilities of test users, psychological testing and assessment, educational testing and assessment, testing in employment and credentialing, plus testing in program evaluation and public policy.

Evaluation Standards

In the field of evaluation, and in particular educational evaluation, the Joint Committee on Standards for Educational Evaluation has published three sets of standards for evaluations. *The Personnel Evaluation Standards* was published in 1988, *The Program Evaluation Standards* (2nd edition) was published in 1994, and *The Student Evaluation Standards* was published in 2003.

Each publication presents and elaborates a set of standards for use in a variety of educational settings. The standards provide guidelines for designing, implementing, assessing and improving the identified form of evaluation. Each of the standards has been placed in one of four fundamental categories to promote educational evaluations that are proper, useful, feasible, and accurate. In these sets of standards, validity and reliability considerations are covered under the accuracy topic. For example, the student accuracy standards help ensure that student evaluations will provide sound, accurate, and credible information about student learning and performance.

Controversy

Concerns over how best to apply assessment practices across public school systems have largely focused on questions about the use of high stakes testing and standardized tests, often used to gauge student progress, teacher quality, and school-, district-, or state-wide educational success.

No Child Left Behind

For most researchers and practitioners, the question is not whether tests should be administered at all—there is a general consensus that, when administered in useful ways, tests can offer useful information about student progress and curriculum implementation, as well as offering formative uses for learners. The real issue, then, is whether testing practices as currently implemented can provide these services for educators and students. In the U.S., the No Child Left Behind Act mandates standardized testing nationwide. These tests align with state curriculum and link teacher, student, district, and state accountability to the results of these tests. Proponents of NCLB argue that it offers a tangible method of gauging educational success, holding teachers and schools accountable for failing scores, and closing the achievement gap across class and ethnicity.

Opponents of standardized testing dispute these claims, arguing that holding educators accountable for test results leads to the practice of "teaching to the test." Additionally, many argue that the focus on standardized testing encourages teachers to equip students with a narrow set of skills that enhance test performance without actually fostering a deeper understanding of subject matter or key principles within a knowledge domain.

High Stakes Testing Practices

The assessments which have caused the most controversy in the US are the use of High school graduation examinations, which first appeared to support the defunct Certificate of Initial Mastery, which can be used to deny diplomas to students who do not meet high standards. They argue that one measure should not be the sole determinant of success or failure. Technical notes for standards based assessments such as Washington's WASL warn that such tests lack the reliability needed to use scores for individual decisions, yet the state legislature passed a law requiring that the WASL be used for just such a purpose. Others such as Washington State University's Don Orlich question the use of test items far beyond standard cognitive levels for testing ages, and the use of expensive, holistically graded tests to measure the quality of both the system and individuals for very large numbers of students.

High stakes tests, even when they do not invoke punishment, have been cited for causing sickness and anxiety in students and teachers, and narrowing the curriculum towards test preparation. In an exercise designed to make children comfortable about testing, a Spokane, Washington newspaper published a picture of a monster that feeds on fear. The published image is purportedly the response of a student who was asked to draw a picture of what she thought of the state assessment. Such high-stakes testing, however, is thought to be acceptable if it increases student learning outcomes.

Standardized multiple choice tests do not conform to the latest education standards. Nevertheless, they are much less expensive, less prone to disagreement between scorers, and can be scored quickly enough to be returned before the end of the school year. Legislation such as No Child Left Behind also define failure if a school does not show improvement from year to year, even if the school is already successful. The use of IQ tests has been banned in some states for educational decisions, and norm referenced tests have been criticized for bias against minorities. Yet the use of standards based assessments to make high stakes decisions, with greatest impact falling on low-scoring ethnic groups, is widely supported by education officials because they show the achievement gap which is promised to be closed merely by implementing standards based education reform. Many states are currently using testing practices which have been condemned by dissenting education experts such as Fairtest and Alfie Kohn.

21st Century Assessment

It has been widely noted that with the emergence of social media and Web 2.0 technologies and mindsets, learning is increasingly collaborative and knowledge increasingly distributed across many members of a learning community. Traditional assessment practices, however, focus in large part on the individual and fail to account for knowledge-building and learning in context. As researchers in the field of assessment consider the cultural shifts that arise from the emergence of a more participatory culture, they will need to find new methods of applying assessments to learners."

13
Glossary of Education

This glossary of education-related terms is based on how they commonly are used.

- **.edu:** ("dot-edu") The generic top-level domain for educational institutions, primarily those in the United States. Created in January 1985 as one of the first top-level domains, .edu was originally intended for educational institutions anywhere in the world.

  With few exceptions, however, only those in the United States registered such domains, while educational institutions in other countries usually used domain names under the appropriate country code TLD.

A

- **Academia:** A collective term for the scientific and cultural community engaged in higher education and research, taken as a whole. The word comes from the *akademeia* just outside ancient Athens, where the *gymnasium* was made famous by Plato as a center of learning.
- **Academic degree:** A degree is any of a wide range of status levels conferred by institutions of higher education, such as universities, normally as the result of successfully completing a program of study.

- **Academic dress:** (or academical dress, also known in the United States as academic regalia) Traditional clothing worn specifically in academic settings. It is more commonly seen nowadays only at graduation ceremonies, but in former times academic dress was, and to a lesser extent in many ancient universities still is, worn on a daily basis.

- **Academic institution:** An educational institution dedicated to higher education and research, which grants academic degrees.

- **Academic publishing:** Describes a system of publishing that is necessary in order for academic scholars to review work and make it available for a wider audience. The "system," which is probably disorganized enough not to merit the title, varies widely by field, and is also always changing, if often slowly. Most academic work is published in journal article or book form.

- **Active learning:** A process whereby learners are actively engaged in the learning process, rather than "passively" absorbing lectures. Active learning involves reading, writing, discussion, and engagement in solving problems, analysis, synthesis, and evaluation. Active learning often involves cooperative learning.

- **Additional Support Needs:** In Scotland, children who require some additional support to remove barriers to learning in any respect are deemed to have Additional Support Needs. This definition abolished the previously used term Special Educational Needs and was set out in the 2004 Additional Support for Learning Act.

- **Adult education:** The practice of teaching and educating adults. This is often done in the workplace, or through 'extension' or 'continuing education' courses at secondary schools, or at a College or University. The practice is also often referred to as 'Training and Development'. It has also been referred to as *andragogy* (to distinguish it from *pedagogy*).

Educating adults differs from educating children in several ways. One of the most important differences is that adults have accumulated knowledge and experience which can either add value to a learning experience or hinder it.

- **Agricultural education:** Instruction about crop production, livestock management, soil and water conservation, and various other aspects of agriculture. Agricultural education includes instruction in food education, such as nutrition. Agricultural and food education improves the quality of life for all people by helping farmers increase production, conserve resources, and provide nutritious foods.
- **Analysis:** The action of taking something apart in order to study it.
- **Applied academics:** An approach to learning and teaching that focuses on how academic subjects (communications, mathematics, science, and basic literacy) can apply to the real world. Further, applied academics can be viewed as theoretical knowledge supporting practical applications.
- **Apprenticeship:** A traditional method, still popular in some countries, of training a new generation of skilled crafts practitioners. Apprentices (or in early modern usage "prentices") built their careers from apprenticeships.
- **Assessment:** The process of documenting, usually in measurable terms, knowledge, skills, attitudes and beliefs.

- **Autodidacticism:** (also autodidactism) Self-education or self-directed learning. An autodidact, also known as an automath, is a mostly self-taught person - typically someone who has an enthusiasm for self-education and a high degree of self-motivation.

B

- **Behaviorism:** (or behaviourism, not to be confused with behavioralism in political science) An approach to psychology based on the proposition that behavior can be researched scientifically without recourse to inner mental states. It is a form of materialism, denying any independent significance for the mind.

  One of the assumptions of many behaviorists is that free will is illusory, and that all behaviour is determined by a combination of forces both genetic factors and the environment, either through association or reinforcement.

- **Bias in education:** A real or perceived bias in the educational system.

- **Bilingual education:** Has multiple definitions:

  - education where two distinct languages are used for general teaching;

  - education designed to help children become bilingual;

  - education in a child's native language for (a) the first year or (b) however long it takes; followed by mainstreaming in English-only classes (in the US);

  - education in a child's native language for as long as his parents wish.

  In the latter cases "native-language instruction" may be a clearer definition.

- **Boarding school:** A school where some or all students not only study but also live, amongst their peers but away from their home and family. The word 'boarding' is used in the sense of a 'boarding house', lodgings which provide both bed and board, that is meals as well as a room. Most famous UK public schools are boarding schools for ages 13 to 18, either single-sex or coeducational.

- **Brainwashing:** (or thought reform) The application of coercive techniques to change the beliefs or behavior of one or more people for political purposes. Whether any techniques at all exist that will actually work to change thought and behavior to the degree that the term "brainwashing" connotes is a controversial and at times hotly debated question.

- **Bridge program:** This is a higher education program specifically designed to assist a student with an attained initial educational level (or an initial level of professional licensure) to attend college courses and achieve a terminal degree (or a higher level of professional licensure) in the same field of study and in less time than an entry-level student would require. Bridge programs are most notable among healthcare professions.

- **Bully:** An individual, thought to be emotionally dysfunctional, who torments others through verbal harassment, physical assault, or other more subtle methods of coercion.

C

- **Chemistry education:** An active area of research within both the disciplines of chemistry and education. The main focus of research is on learning and teaching of chemistry in schools, colleges and universities. The practice of chemical education is teaching chemistry to students and the training of teachers to teach chemistry. The research aspect deals with how to teach and how to improve learning outcomes.

- **Classical conditioning:** (also Pavlovian conditioning or respondent conditioning) A type of associative learning. These associations are formed by pairing two stimuli—what Ivan Pavlov described as the learning of conditioned behavior— to condition an animal to give a certain response. The simplest form of classical conditioning is reminiscent of what Aristotle would have called the law of contiguity which states that: "When two things commonly occur together, the appearance of one will bring the other to mind."
- **Classical education:** May refer to the education of antiquity and the Middle Ages, or the education of later periods based on Classics and Western culture, or the completely different Chinese tradition of education, based in large part on Confucian and Taoist traditions.
- **Classroom management:** A term used by many teachers to describe the process of ensuring lessons run smoothly without disruptive behaviour by students. It is possibly the most difficult aspect of teaching for many teachers and indeed experiencing problems in this area causes many people to leave teaching altogether. It is closely linked to issues of motivation, discipline and respect.
- **Coeducation:** The integrated education of men and women at the same school facilities; co-ed is a shortened adjectival form of co-educational. Before the 1960s, many private institutions of higher education restricted their enrollment to a single sex. Indeed, most institutions of higher education—regardless of being

public or private—restricted their enrollment to a single sex at some point in their history. "Coed" is an informal (and increasingly archaic) term for a female student attending such a college or university.

- **Cognitive relativism:** (also called epistemic or epistemological relativism) A philosophy that claims the truth or falsity of a statement is relative to a social group.
- **College athletics:** Refers to a set of physical activities comprising sports and games put into place by institutions of tertiary education (colleges in American English). In the United States, college athletics is overseen by the National Collegiate Athletic Association and by the National Association of Intercollegiate Athletics. College athletics has a high profile in the United States, and to a lesser extent in Canada, where it is known as interuniversity sport. In the most of the rest of the world the equivalent level of competition is only followed by the competitors and their close friends and families.
- **Community of practice:** (often abbreviated as CoP) Refers to the process of social learning that occurs when people who have a common interest in some subject or problem collaborate over an extended period to share ideas, find solutions, and build innovations.
- **Comparative education:** Seeks to throw light on education in one country (or group of countries) by using data and insights drawn from the practises and situation in another country, or countries.
- **Computer Based Learning:** (sometimes abbreviated CBL) Refers to the use of computers as a key compoent of the educational environment. While this can refer to the use of computers in a classroom, the term more

broadly refers to a structured environment in which computers are used for teaching purposes. The concept is generally seen as being distinct from the use of computers in ways where learning is at least a peripheral element of the experience.

- **Constructivism:** A set of assumptions about the nature of human learning that guide constructivist learning theories and teaching methods. Constructivism values developmentally appropriate, teacher-supported learning that is initiated and directed by the student.
- **Cooperative education:** A structured method of combining academic education with practical work experience. Research indicates that one of the attributes employers value most in newly hired employees is work experience. A cooperative education experience, commonly known as a "co-op", provides academic credit for career work. Cooperative education is taking on new importance in school-to-work transition, service learning, and experiential learning initiatives.
- **Cooperative learning:** Proposed in response to traditional curriculum-driven education. In cooperative learning environments, students interact in purposely structured heterogeneous group to support the learning of one self and others in the same group.
- **Course:** in the United States, a unit of instruction in one subject, lasting one academic term
- **Course of study:** in the British Commonwealth, a programme of education leading to a degree or diploma
- **Creativity:** A human mental phenomenon based around the deployment of mental skills and/or conceptual tools, which, in turn, originate and develop innovation, inspiration, or insight.

- **Creativity techniques:** Heuristic methods to facilitate creativity in a person or a group of people. Generally, most creativity techniques use associations between the goal (or the problem), the current state (which may be an imperfect solution to the problem), and some stimulus (possibly selected randomly). There is an analogy between many creativity techniques and methods of evolutionary computation.

- **Critical pedagogy:** A teaching approach which attempts to help students question and challenge domination, and the beliefs and practices that dominate. In other words, it is a theory and practice of helping students achieve critical consciousness. In this tradition the teacher works to lead students to question ideologies and practices considered oppressive (including those at school), and encourage liberatory collective and individual responses to the actual conditions of their own lives.

- **Critical thinking:** Consists of a mental process of analyzing or evaluating information, particularly statements or propositions that people have offered as true. It forms a process of reflecting upon the meaning of statements, examining the offered evidence and reasoning, and forming judgments about the facts. Critical thinkers can gather such information from observation, experience, reasoning, and/or communication. Critical thinking has its basis in intellectual values that go beyond subject-matter divisions and which include: clarity, accuracy, precision, evidence, thoroughness and fairness.

- **Cultural learning:** The way a group of people within a society or culture tend to learn and pass on new information. Learning styles are greatly influenced by how a culture socializes with its children and young people.

D

- **Distance education:** (or distance learning) A field of education that focuses on the pedagogy/andragogy, technology, and instructional systems design that is effectively incorporated in delivering education to students who are not physically "on site" to receive their education. Instead, teachers and students may communicate asynchronously by exchanging printed or electronic media, or through technology that allows them to communicate in real time (synchronously). Distance education courses that require a physical on-site presence for any reason including the taking of examinations is considered to be a hybrid or blended course or program.
- **Dunce:** A person incapable of learning. The word is derived from the name of the great schoolman, John Duns Scotus, whose works on logic, theology and philosophy were accepted textbooks in the universities from the 14th century.
- **Dyslexia:** Said to be a neurological disorder with biochemical and genetic markers. Dyslexia was originally defined as a difficulty with reading and writing that could not be explained by general intelligence. One diagnostic approach is to compare their ability in areas such as reading and writing to that which would be predicted by his or her general level of intelligence, but some would say that it is not certain that intelligence should be a predictor of reading or writing ability; and also that the causes, effects and treatments of reading disabilities may be similar for all levels of intelligence.

E

- **Early childhood education:** Covers the education of a child from the period from birth to eight years of age.

- **Education:** A social science that encompasses teaching and learning specific knowledge, beliefs, and skills. Licensed and practicing teachers in the field use a variety of methods and materials in order to impart a curriculum.

- **Education policy:** is the collection of rules, both stated and implicit, or the regularities in practice that govern the behavior of persons in schools. Education policy analysis is the scholarly study of education policy.

- **Education reform:** A plan, program, or movement which attempts to bring about a systematic change in educational theory or practice across a community or society.

- **Education voucher:** (commonly called a school voucher) A certificate by which parents are given the ability to pay for the education of their children at a school of their choice, rather than the public school to which they were assigned. These vouchers would be paid for using tax revenues.

- **Educational animation:** Animation produced for the specific purpose of fostering learning.

- **Educational counseling:** Conducted by counselors in schools and universities. It is intended to help children suffering from education-related traumas such as beatings and other forms of corporal punishment used in many countries. A more common application is with children who have been abused or bullied. The counselor works with the child to help him or her get over the trauma he or she has suffered.

- **Educational evaluation:** The evaluation process of characterizing and appraising some aspect of the education enterprise.

- **Educational film:** A film or movie whose primary purpose is to educate. Educational films have been used in classrooms as an alternative to other teaching methods.
- **Educational games:** Games, including video games of this genre, designed to teach people, typically children, about a certain subject or help them learn a skill as they play. Some people call these types of games edutainment because they combine education and entertainment.
- **Educational organization:** Organization within the scope of education. It is a common misconception that this means it is organizing educational system; rather, it deals with the theory of organization as it applies to education of the human mind.
- **Educational programming language:** A programming language that is designed primarily as a learning instrument and not so much as a tool for writing real-world application programs.
- **Educational psychology:** The study of how humans learn in educational settings, the effectiveness of educational treatments, the psychology of teaching, and the social psychology of schools as organizations. Although the terms "educational psychology" and "school psychology" are often used interchangeably, researchers and theorists are likely to be identified as educational psychologists, whereas practitioners in schools or school-related settings are identified as school psychologists. Educational psychology is concerned with the processes of educational attainment among the general population and sub-populations such as gifted children and those subject to specific disabilities.

- **Educational research:** Research conducted to investigate behavioral patterns in pupils, students, teachers and other participants in schools and other educational institutions. Such research is often conducted by examining work products such as documents and standardized test results. The methods of educational research are derived chiefly from the social sciences, and in particular from psychology.
- **Educational software:** Computer software whose primary purpose is teaching or self-learning.
- **Educational technology:** The use of technology to improve education. It is a systematic, iterative process for designing instruction or training used to improve performance. Educational technology is sometimes also known as instructional technology or learning technology.
- **E-learning:** An approach to facilitate and enhance learning through, and based on, both computer and communications technology. Such devices can include personal computers, CDROMs, Digital Television, P.D.A.s and Mobile Phones. Communications technology enables the use of the Internet, email, discussion forums, collaborative software and team learning systems.
- **Electronic portfolio:** In the context of education and learning, an electronic portfolio, normally known as an ePortfolio or a digital portfolio, is a portfolio based on electronic media and services. It consists of a personal digital record containing information such as a collection of artifacts or evidence demonstrating what one knows and can do.
- **Engagement:** The sentiment a student feels or does not feel towards learning or the learning environment.

- **Experience:** Comprises knowledge of or skill in or observation of some thing or some event gained through involvement in or exposure to that thing or event. The history of the word *experience* aligns it closely with the concept of *experiment*.

  The concept of experience generally refers to know-how or procedural knowledge, rather than propositional knowledge. Philosophers dub knowledge based on experience "empirical knowledge" or "*a posteriori* knowledge". A person with considerable experience in a certain field can gain a reputation as an expert.

- **Experiential education:** (or "learning by doing") The process of actively engaging students in an authentic experience that will have benefits and consequences. Students make discoveries and experiment with knowledge themselves instead of hearing or reading about the experiences of others. Students also reflect on their experiences, thus developing new skills, new attitudes, and new theories or ways of thinking. Experiential education is related to the constructivist learning theory.

- **Experimental analysis of behavior:** The name given to the approach to psychology founded by B. F. Skinner. As its name suggests, its foundational principle was the rejection of theoretical analysis, in particular the kinds of learning theory that had grown up in the comparative psychology of the 1920-1950 period, in favor of a more direct approach. It owed its early success to the effectiveness of Skinner's procedure of operant conditioning, both in the laboratory and in behavior therapy.

- **Expulsion** (academia): Removing a student from a school or university for violating rules or honor codes.

- **Extra credit** is an academic concept, particularly used in schools. Students are offered the opportunity to undertake optional work, additional to their compulsory school work, in order to gain additional credit that would boost their grades.

- **Extracurricular activities:** Activities performed by students that fall outside the realm of the normal curriculum of school or university education. Extracurricular activities exist at all levels of education, from high school and college to university education. Such activities are generally voluntary as opposed to mandatory, non-paying, tend to be social or philanthropic as opposed to scholastic, and involve others of the same age. Students often organize and direct these activities under faculty sponsorship.

F

- **Forbidden knowledge:** (in contrast to secret knowledge) Used to describe forbidden books or other information to which access is restricted or deprecated for political or religious reasons. Forbidden knowledge is commonly not secret, rather a society or various institutions will use repressive mechanisms to either completely prevent the publication of information they find objectionable or dangerous (censorship), or failing that, to try to reduce the public's trust in such information (propaganda). Public repression can create paradoxical situation where the proscribed information is generally common knowledge but publicly citing it is disallowed.

- **Functional illiteracy:** Refers to the inability of an individual to use reading, speaking, writing, and computational skills efficiently in everyday life situations. Unlike an illiterate, a functionally illiterate adult could be able to read and write text in his native language, but is unable like the first, even in his own cultural and linguistic environment, to perform such fundamental tasks as filling out an application for employment, following written instructions, reading a newspaper, reading traffic signs, consulting a dictionary, or understanding a bus schedule.

- **Future Problem Solving Program:** (FPSP) An international academic competition. Over 250,000 students internationally participate in the Future Problem Solving program every year. Participating countries include the United States, Canada, Australia, New Zealand, Korea, Malaysia, Russia, Hong Kong and Singapore.

G

- **Gifted education:** is a broad term for special practices, procedures and theories used in the education of children who have been identified as gifted or talented. Youths are usually identified as gifted by placing highly on certain standardized tests.

  Advocates of gifted education argue that gifted and/or talented youth are so perceptually and intellectually above the mean, it is appropriate to pace their lessons more aggressively, track them into honors, Advanced Placement, or International Baccalaureate courses, or otherwise provide educational enrichment.

- **Gymnasia and Realgymnasia:** (singular: Gymnasium) and Realgymnasia were the classical higher or secondary schools of Germany from the sixteenth century to the twentieth century. Students were admitted at 9 or 10 years of age and were required to have a knowledge of reading, writing, and arithmetic.

H

- **Habituation:** An example of non-associative learning in which there is a progressive diminution of behavioral response probability with repetition of a stimulus. It is another form of integration.

- **Higher education:** Education provided by universities and other institutions that award academic degrees, such as community colleges, and liberal arts colleges.

  Higher education includes both the teaching and the research activities of universities, and within the realm of teaching, it includes both the *undergraduate* level (sometimes referred to as tertiary education) and the *graduate* (or *postgraduate*) level (sometimes referred to as quaternary education or graduate school). Higher education differs from other forms of post-secondary education such as vocational education. However, most professional education is included within higher education, and many postgraduate qualifications are strongly vocationally or professionally oriented, for example in disciplines such as law and medicine.

- **Homeschooling:** (also home education or home school) An educational alternative in which children are educated at home and in the community, in contrast to a compulsory education which takes place in an institution such as a publicly-run or privately run school. Home education methods are similar to those widely used before the popularization of compulsory education in the 19th century. Before this time, the majority of education worldwide was provided at home by family and community members, with only the privileged attending privately run schools or employing tutors, the only available alternatives at the time.

I

- **Individualized instruction:** A method of instruction in which content, instructional materials, instructional media, and pace of learning are based upon the abilities and interests of each individual learner.
- **Inquiry education:** (sometimes known as the inquiry method) A student-centered method of education focused on asking questions. Students are encouraged to ask questions which are meaningful to them, and which do not necessarily have easy answers; teachers are encouraged to avoid speaking at all when this is possible, and in any case to avoid giving answers in favor of asking more questions.
- **Instructional capital:** A term used in educational administration after the 1960s, to reflect capital resulting from investment in producing learning materials.
- **Instructional design:** (also known as instructional systems design) The analysis of learning needs and systematic development of instruction. Instructional designers often use instructional technology as a method for developing instruction. Instructional design models typically specify a method, that if followed will facilitate the transfer of knowledge, skills and attitude to the recipient or acquirer of the instruction.
- **Instructional scaffolding:** The provision of sufficient supports to promote learning when concepts and skills are being first introduced to students.
- **Instructional technology:** Born as a military response to the problems of a labor shortage during WWII in the United States. There was a definitive need to fill

the factories with skilled labor. Instructional technology provided a methodology for training in a systematic and efficient manner.

- **Integrative learning:** A learning theory describing a movement toward integrated lessons helping students make connections across curricula. This higher education concept is distinct from the elementary and high school "integrated curriculum" movement.

- **Intelligence (trait):** The mental capacity to reason, plan, solve problems, think abstractly, comprehend ideas and language, and learn. Although nonscientists generally regard the concept of intelligence as having much broader scope, in psychology, the study of intelligence generally regards this trait as distinct from creativity, personality, character, or wisdom.

- **International education:** The practice and/or study of international cooperation and aid among countries, including the exchange of students, teachers, and researchers between countries. International education is connected to comparative education.

- **Intrinsic motivation:** Evident when people engage in an activity for its own sake, without some obvious external incentive present. A hobby is a typical example.

- **Invigilator:** Someone who ensures the smooth running of exams. An invigilator is responsible for ensuring that the Awarding Body's regulations are complied with; that exams start and finish at the correct time; that exam papers are secure whilst in their care; that attendance and seating plans are recorded; and that no cheating takes place. The invigilator will also deal with any problems that arise during an exam, including emergency evacuations, and ensure that no unauthorised materials are present, including mobile phones.

J

- **Joint Committee on Standards for Educational Evaluation:** A coalition of major professional associations formed in 1975 to help improve the quality of evaluation. The Joint Committee published three sets of standards for evaluations. *The Personnel Evaluation Standards* was published in 1988, *The Program Evaluation Standards* (2nd edition) was published in 1994, and *The Student Evaluations Standards* was published in 2003.

K

- **Kindergarten:** (German for *garden for children*) A name used in many parts of the world for the first stages of a child's classroom education. In some parts kindergarten is part of the formal school system; in others it may refer to pre-school or daycare.
- **Kinesthetic learning:** A teaching and learning style in which learning takes place by the student actually carrying out a physical activity, rather than listening to a lecture or merely watching a demonstration. Building dioramas, physical models or participating in role-playing or historical reenactment are some examples. Other examples include the kindergarten practice of having children perform various motions from left to right in preparation for reading education.
- **Knowledge Management:** (or KM) A term applied to techniques used for the systematic collection, transfer, security and management of information within organisations, along with systems designed to help make best use of that knowledge. In particular it refers to tools and techniques designed to preserve the availability of information held by key individuals and facilitate decision making and reducing risk.

- **Knowledge representation:** (KR) Most commonly used to refer to representations intended for processing by modern computers, and particularly for representations consisting of explicit objects.

- **Knowledge transfer:** In the fields of Organizational development and organizational learning, is the practical problem of getting a packet of knowledge from one part of the organization to another (or all other) parts of the organization. It is considered to be more than just a communications problem.

L

- **Language education:** The teaching and learning of a language or languages, usually as foreign languages.

- **Law (principle):** Refers to universal principles that describe the fundamental nature of something, to universal properties and relationships between things, or to descriptions that purport to explain these principles and relationships.

- **Learning:** The process of acquiring knowledge, skills, attitudes, or values, through study, experience, or teaching, that causes a change of behavior that is persistent, measurable, and specified or allows an individual to formulate a new mental construct or revise a prior mental construct (conceptual knowledge such as attitudes or values). It is a process that depends on experience and leads to long-term changes in behavior potential.

- **Learning by teaching (LdL):** In professional education (in German "Lernen durch Lehren", therefore LdL) designates a method which allows pupils and students to prepare and teach lessons or parts of lessons. Learning by teaching should not be confused with presentations or lectures by students, as students do not only convey a certain content, but choose their own methodological and didactical approach in teaching their classmates a certain area of the respective subject.

- **Learning disability:** In the United States, the term learning disability is used to refer to socio-biological conditions that affect a persons communicative capacities and potential to learn. The term includes conditions such as perceptual disability, brain injury, minimal brain dysfunction, autism, dyslexia, and developmental aphasia. In the United Kingdom, the term learning disability is used more generally to refer to developmental disability.
- **Legal education:** The education of individuals who intend to become legal professionals (attorneys and judges) or those who simply intend to use their law degree to some end, either related to law (such as politics or academic) or unrelated (such as business entrepreneurship).
- **Lesson plan:** A teacher's detailed description of the course of instruction for an individual lesson. While there is no one way to construct a correct lesson plan, most lesson plans contain similar elements.
- **Liberal arts:** Studies that are intended to provide general knowledge and intellectual skills, rather than more specialized occupational or professional skills.
- **Lifelong learning:** The concept that "It's never too soon or too late for learning", a philosophy that has taken root in a whole host of different organizations. Lifelong learning sees citizens provided with learning opportunities at all ages and in numerous contexts: at work, at home and through leisure activities, not just through formal channels such as school and higher education.

- **Literacy:** The ability to read and write. In modern context, the word means reading and writing in a level adequate for written communication and generally a level that enables one to successfully function at certain levels of a socie

M

- **Mastery learning:** An instructional method that presumes all children can learn if they are provided with the appropriate learning conditions. Specifically, mastery learning is a method whereby students are not advanced to a subsequent learning objective until they demonstrate proficiency with the current one.

- **MEB:** A Master in European Business providing knowledge and skills both in Economics and Management.

- **Mathematics education:** The study of practices and methods of both the teaching and learning of mathematics. Furthermore, mathematics educators are concerned with the development of tools that facilitate practice and/or the study of practice. Mathematics education has been a hotly debated subject in modern society. There is an ambiguity in the term for it refers both to these practices in classrooms around the world, but also to an emergent discipline with its own journals, conferences, etc. The main international body involved is the International Commission on Mathematical Instruction.

- **Medical education:** Education related to the practice of being a medical practitioner, either the initial training to become a doctor or further training thereafter.

  Medical education and training varies considerably across the world. Various teaching methodologies have been utilised in medical education, which is an active area of educational research.

- **Memory:** The ability of the brain to store, retain, and subsequently recall information. Although traditional studies of memory began in the realms of philosophy, the late nineteenth and early twentieth century put memory within the paradigms of cognitive psychology. In the recent decades, it has become one of the principal pillars of a new branch of science that represents a marriage between cognitive psychology and neuroscience, called cognitive neuroscience.
- **Medieval university (Asia):** Medieval universities did not exist in Asia in the strict sense of the phrase. However, there were important centres of learning that can be compared to the universities of Europe. It must be noted that unlike the European universities, non-western institutions of higher learning were never known to issue degrees to their graduates and therefore do not meet what many hold to be the technical definition of university. This does not, however, bar their importance to the history of non-western cultures.
- **Meta-:** In epistemology, the prefix meta- is used to mean *about (its own category)*. For example, metadata is data about data (who has produced it, when, what format the data is in and so on). Similarly, meta-memory in psychology means an individual's intuition about whether or not they would remember something if they concentrated on recalling it. Any subject can be said to have a *meta-theory,* which is the theoretical consideration of its foundations and methods.
- **Metacognition:** Refers to thinking about cognition (memory, perception, calculation, association, etc.)

itself. Metacognition can be divided into two types of knowledge: explicit, conscious, factual knowledge; and implicit, unconscious, procedural knowledge.

- **Methodology:** Strictly speaking is the study and knowledge of methods; but the term is frequently used pretentiously to indicate a method or a set of methods. In other words, it is the study of techniques for problem-solving and seeking answers, as opposed to the techniques themselves.
- **Military education and training:** A process which intends to establish and improve the capabilities of military personnel in their respective roles.
- **Mind map:** (or mind-map) A diagram used for linking words and ideas to a central key word or idea. It is used to visualize, classify, structure, and generate ideas, as well as an aid in study, problem solving, and decision making.
- **Motivation:** The driving force behind all actions of human beings and other animals. It is an internal state that activates behavior and gives it direction. Emotion is closely related to motivation, and may be regarded as the subjectively experienced component of motivational states.
- **Music education:** Comprises the application of education methods in teaching music.

N

- **NAACP Legal Defense and Educational Fund, Inc.:** (NAACP LDF or simply LDF) A leading United States civil rights organization. It was founded in 1940 under the leadership of Thurgood Marshall as part of the National Association for the Advancement of Colored People (NAACP) and spun out as a separate organization in 1957.

- **National Educational Television:** (NET) was an educational television network in the USA from 1952 until 1970 and was the predecessor of the Public Broadcasting Service.

- **Nines System:** The informal name for a grading scale often used at educational institutions in English-speaking countries, particularly the United States.

  The system owes its name to the fact that each of the top four letter grades in it cover a range of nine points. The minimum passing mark under it is almost always 65%, or five points higher than in the more widely-used Tens System.

- **Normal school:** An educational institution for training teachers. Its purpose is to establish teaching standards or *norms*, hence its name. The term *normal school* is now archaic in all but a few countries. In New Zealand, for example, normal schools are affiliated with Teachers colleges. According to the *Oxford English Dictionary*, normal schools in the United States and Canada trained primary school teachers, while in Europe, normal schools educated primary, secondary and tertiary-level teachers.

- **Numeracy:** A term that emerged in the United Kingdom as a contraction of "numerical literacy". In the United States, it is somewhat better known as "Quantitative Literacy," and is familiar to math educators and intellectuals but not in the common usage. Innumeracy is the absence of numeracy.

O

- **Objectivity** (philosophy): Has various meanings in philosophy, and is surely one of the most important philosophical problems, since it concerns the epistemological status of knowledge, the problem of an objective reality and the question of our subjective relationship to others objects in the world.

- **Obscurantism:** Opposition to extension or dissemination of knowledge beyond certain limits and to questioning dogmas. Obscurantism is the opposite of freethought and is often associated with religious fundamentalism by its opponents. Indeed, it is a commonly raised accusation in debates on academic freedom, with anti-communists and others associating it with the philosophy of G. W. F. Hegel and his followers (including Karl Marx) and more recently with opponents of Martin Heidegger doing the same.
- **Observation:** An activity of an sapient or sentient living being, which senses and assimiliate the knowledge of a phenomenon in its framework of previous knowledge and ideas.
- **Open problem:** A problem that can be formally stated and for which a solution is known to exist but which has not yet been solved. It is common in graduate schools to point out open problems to students.
- **Operant conditioning:** (so named by psychologist B. F. Skinner) The modification of behavior brought about over time by the consequences of said behavior. *Operant conditioning* is distinguished from Pavlovian conditioning in that operant conditioning deals with voluntary behavior explained by its consequences, while Pavlovian conditioning deals with involuntary behavior triggered by its antecedents.
- **Outdoor education:** (also known as adventure education) Usually refers to organized learning that takes place in the outdoors. Programs often involve residential or journey-based experiences in which students participate in a variety of adventurous

challenges such as hiking, climbing, canoeing, ropes courses, and group games. Outdoor education programs draw upon the philosophy and theory of experiential education and may also focus on environmental education.

P

- **Peace education:** The process of acquiring the knowledge and developing the attitudes, skills, and behaviour to live in harmony with oneself and with others.

- **Pedagogy:** The art or science of teaching. The word comes from the ancient Greek *paidagogos*, the slave who took little boys to and from school as part of paideia. The word "paidia" refers to children, which is why some like to make the distinction between pedagogy (teaching children) and andragogy (teaching adults). The Latin word for pedagogy, education, is much more widely used, and often the two are used interchangeably.

- **Philosophy of education:** The study of the purpose, nature and ideal content of education. Other questions include the nature of the knowing mind and the human subject, problems of authority, the relationship between education and society, etc. At least since Rousseau's time, the philosophy of education has been linked to theories of developmental psychology and human development.

- **Physical education:** A course in the curriculum which utilizes the learning medium of large-muscle activities in a play or movement exploration setting. It is almost always mandatory for students in elementary schools, and often for students in middle schools and high schools.

- **Physics education:** A relatively new, yet active, area of research within the science of physics. The main focus of research is on learning and teaching of physics in both the highschool and college level.
- **Postgraduate education:** (or Quaternary education) The fourth-stage educational level, and follows the completion of an undergraduate degree at a college or university. Graduate school is an example of quaternary education; some consider *masters-level* degrees as part of tertiary education; some consider postdoctoral positions to be quaternary education while others consider them to be jobs.
- **Post-secondary education:** Any form of education that is taken after first attending a secondary school, such as a high school. The purpose of a post-secondary education can be to receive vocational education and training or to prepare for professions or scientific/ academic careers through higher education.
- **Primary education:** (or elementary education) Consists of the first years of formal, structured education that occurs during childhood. In most countries, it is compulsory for children to receive primary education (though in many jurisdictions it is permissible for parents to provide it). Primary education generally begins when children are four to seven years of age. The division between primary and secondary education is somewhat arbitrary, but it generally occurs at about twelve years of age (adolescence); some educational systems have separate middle schools for that period.
- **Problem finding:** Problem discovery. It is part of the larger problem process that includes problem shaping and problem solving. Problem finding requires

intellectual vision and insight into what is missing. This involves the application of creativity.

- **Problem shaping:** Revising a question so that the solution process can begin or continue. It is part of the larger problem process that includes problem finding and problem solving. Problem shaping (or problem framing) often involves the application of critical thinking.

- **Problem solving:** Forms part of thinking. It occurs if an organism or an artificial intelligence system does not know how to proceed from a given state to a desired goal state. It is part of the larger problem process that includes problem finding and problem shaping.

- **Professional certification:** (trade certification, or professional designation often called simply certification or qualification) A designation earned by a person to certify that he is qualified to perform a job. Certification indicates that the individual has a specific knowledge, skills, or abilities in the view of the certifying body. Professional certifications are awarded by professional bodies and corporations. The difference between licensure and certification is licensure is required by law, whereas certification is generally voluntary. Sometimes the word *certification* is used for *licensure.*

- **Programmed instruction:** A field first studied extensively by the behaviorist B.F. Skinner. It consists of teaching through small lessons, where each lesson must be mastered in order to go on to the next. Students work through the programmed material by themselves at their own speed. After each step, they are presented with a question to test their comprehension, then are immediately shown the correct answer or given additional information.

- **Public school:** The term has different (and in some cases contradictory) meanings due to regional differences.
- **Pygmalion effect:** (or Rosenthal effect) refers to situations in which students perform better than other students simply because they are expected to do so.

Q

- **Quiz:** A form of game or puzzle in which the players (as individuals or in teams), attempt to answer questions correctly. A quiz usually is a form of student assessment, but often has fewer questions of lesser difficulty and requires less time for completion than a test.

R

- **Reading** (activity): The process of retrieving and comprehending some form of stored information or ideas. These ideas are usually some sort of representation of language, as symbols to be examined by sight, or by touch (for example Braille). Other types of reading may not be language-based, such as music notation or pictograms. By analogy, in computer science, reading is acquiring of data from some sort of computer storage.
- **Reading disability:** A condition in which a sufferer displays difficulty reading resulting primarily from neurological factors.
- **Reading education:** There are basically two different common methods of teaching reading. One usually refers to whole language approach ("look say"), the other usually refers to phonetics approach. The tension between these two approaches is often referred to as "the great debate".

- **Reason:** A term used in philosophy and other human sciences to refer to the higher cognitive faculties of the human mind. It describes a type of thought or aspect of thought, especially abstract thought, and the ability to think abstractly, which is felt to be especially human.

- **Recitation:** A discussion carried by a Teaching Assistant to supplement a lecture given by a senior faculty at an academic institution. During the recitation, TAs will review the lecture, expand on the concepts, and carry a discussion with the students.

- **Reference:** Something that refers or points to something else, or acts as a connection or a link between two things. The objects it links may be concrete, such as books or locations, or abstract, such as data, thoughts, or memories. The object which is named by a reference, or to which the reference points, is the referent.

- **Reinforcement:** In operant conditioning, reinforcement is any change in an organism's surroundings that: occurs regularly when the organism behaves in a given way (that is, is contingent on a specific response); and is associated with an increase in the probability that the response will be made or in another measure of its strength.

- **Religious education:** Teaches the doctrines of a religion. Its usual purpose is to teach children the basics of a religion. A less common purpose is to teach new adherents of a religion.

  Since people within a given country often hold varying religious and non-religious beliefs, government-sponsored religious education can be a source of conflict. Those that allow it also vary in the type of education provided.

- **Research:** Often described as an active, diligent, and systematic process of inquiry aimed at discovering, interpreting and revising facts. This intellectual investigation produces a greater understanding of events, behaviors, or theories, and makes practical applications through laws and theories. The term *research* is also used to describe a collection of information about a particular subject, and is usually associated with science and the scientific method.

- **Rhodes Scholarships:** Created by Cecil Rhodes and have been awarded to applicants annually since 1902 by the Oxford-based Rhodes Trust on the basis of academic qualities, as well as those of character. They provide the successful candidate with two years of study at the University of Oxford in England, possibly extended for a third year.

  When Rhodes died in 1902, his will stipulated that the greater part of his fortune was to go toward the establishment of a scholarship fund to reward applicants who exhibited worthy qualities of intellect, character, and physical ability.

- **Rote learning:** A learning technique which avoids grasping the inner complexities and inferences of the subject that is being learned and instead focuses on memorizing the material so that it can be recalled by the learner exactly the way it was read or heard.

- **Rubrics** (education): In education, a rubric is a set of criteria and standards linked to learning objectives that is used to assess a student's performance, such as on a paper, project, or essay.

S

- **School:** A place designated for learning. The range of institutions covered by the term varies from country to country.

- **School discipline:** A form of discipline found in schools. The term refers to students complying with a code of behaviour often known as the school rules. Among other things these rules may set out the expected standards of clothing, timekeeping, social behaviour and work ethic.
- **School psychologist:** A practitioner who applies his psychological training to assess and help school children.
- **Science education:** The field concerned with sharing science content and process with individuals not traditionally considered part of the scientific community. The target individuals may be children, college students, or adults within the general public. The field of science education comprises science content, some sociology, and some teaching pedagogy.
- **Science fair:** Generally a competition where contestants create a project related to science or some scientific phenomenon. Science fairs usually are involved with children and schooling; however, the term can be used to describe science fairs independent of the age of the contestants involved. They are often also combined with competition in mathematics or history.
- **Secondary education:** is a period of education which, in most contemporary educational systems of the world, follows directly after primary education, and which may be followed by tertiary, "post-secondary", or "higher" education (e.g., university).
- **Self-concept:** (or self-identity) The mental and conceptual awareness and persistent regard that sentient beings hold with regard their own being. Components of a being's self-concept include physical, psychological, and social attributes; and can be

influenced by its attitudes, habits, beliefs and ideas. These components and attributes can each be condensed to the general concepts of self-image and the self-esteem.

- **Self-efficacy:** The belief that one has the capabilities to execute the courses of actions required to manage prospective situations.
- **Self-esteem:** (or self-worth) Includes a person's subjective appraisal of himself or herself as intrinsically positive or negative to some degree.
- **Service learning:** A method of teaching, learning and reflecting that combines academic classroom curriculum with meaningful youth service throughout the community. As a teaching methodology, it falls under the category of experiential education.
- **Sex education:** Education about sexual reproduction in human beings, sexual intercourse and other aspects of human sexual behavior.
- **Situated learning:** Education that takes place in a setting functionally identical to that where the learning will be applied.
- **Skill:** An ability, usually learned, to perform actions.
- **Sociology of knowledge:** The study of the social origins of ideas, and of the effects prevailing ideas have on societies.
- **Sociology of scientific knowledge:** (SSK) Closely related to the sociology of science, considers social influences on science. Practitioners have engaged in controversy concerning the role that social factors play in scientific development relative to rational, empirical and other factors.

- **Socratic method:** A dialectic method of inquiry, largely applied to the examination of key moral concepts and first described by Plato in the *Socratic Dialogues*. For this, Socrates is customarily regarded as the father and fountainhead for ethics or moral philosophy.
- **Special education:**, describes an educational alternative that focuses on the teaching of students with academic, behaviorial, health, or physical needs that cannot sufficiently be met using traditional educational programs or techniques.
- **Sphere of knowledge:** A unified body or collection of knowledge regarding a specific subject, interest or otherwise area of expertise possessed by an individual.
- **STEM fields:** The Science, Technology, Engineering, and Mathematics (STEM) fields are collectively considered core technological underpinnings of an advanced society. In many forums (including political/governmental and academic) the strength of the STEM workforce is viewed as an indicator of a nation's ability to sustain itself. Maintaining healthy levels of its citizenry well versed in the STEM fields is a key portion of the public education agenda of the United States of America at all levels, and substantial lobbying is underway in Washington, DC to raise awareness of STEM education issues.
- **Stipend:** A form of payment or salary, such as for an internship or apprenticeship. Stipends are usually lower than what would be expected as a permanent salary for similar work. This is because the stipend is complemented by other benefits such as instruction, work experience, food, accommodation, and personal satisfaction. Universities usually refer to monies paid to graduate research assistants as a stipend, rather than as wages, to reflect complementary benefits.

- **Student activism:** A form of youth-led community organizing that is specifically oriented towards engaging students as activists in order to create change in the educational system.
- **Student-centered learning:** An approach to education focusing on the needs of the students, rather than those of others involved in the educational process, such as teachers and administrators. This approach has many implications for the design of curriculum, course content, and interactivity of courses.
- **Student voice:** the distinct perspectives and actions of young people throughout schools focused on education itself.
- **Student loans:** Loans offered to students to assist in payment of the costs of professional education. These loans usually carry lower interests than other loans, and are usually issued by the government.
- **Student organization:** A voluntary association of students at institutions of secondary and higher education for a specific legal purpose. Such organizations are often sponsored through and receive funding from a student government.
- **Syllabus:** (plural *syllabi* or *syllabuses*) A document with an outline and summary of topics to be covered in a course. It is often either set out by an exam board, or prepared by the professor who teaches the course, and is usually given to each student during the first class session.
- **Synthesis:** Placing, is commonly understood to be an integration of two or more pre-existing elements which results in a new creation.

T

- *Taxonomy of Educational Objectives:* An educational taxonomy that classifies educational objectives into three domains: cognitive, affective, and psychomotor.
- **Technology education:** The study of the human ability to create and use tools to shape the natural environment to meet their needs. The goal of technology education is to spread technological literacy or in some countries technacy, which is accomplished by bringing laboratory activities to students. The term "technology education" is frequently shortened to "tech ed".
- **Technology Integration:** A term used by educators to describe effective uses of technology by teachers and students in K-12 and university classrooms. Teachers use technology to support instruction in language arts, social studies, science, math, or other content areas. When teachers integrate technology into their classroom practice, learners are empowered to be actively engaged in their learning.
- **Tertiary education:** The educational level following the completion of a school providing a secondary education such as a high school, secondary school, or gymnasium. Tertiary education is commonly higher education which prepares students for a quaternary education.
- **Theory of cognitive development:** A developmental psychology theory developed by Jean Piaget to explain cognitive development. The theory is central to child psychology and is based on schemata—schemes of how one perceives the world—in "critical periods," times when children are particularly susceptible to certain information.

- **Theory of multiple intelligences:** A psychological and educational theory formulated by Howard Gardner espousing that eight kinds of "intelligence" exist in humans, each relating to a different sphere of human life and activity.

- **Training:** Refers to the acquisition of knowledge, skills, attitudes as a result of the teaching of vocational or practical skills and knowledge and relates to specific useful skills. It forms the core of apprenticeships and provides the backbone of content at technical colleges or polytechnics.

- **Truth:** When someone sincerely agrees with an assertion, he or she is claiming that it is the truth. Philosophy seeks answers for certain questions about truth and the word *truth*.

- **Tuition:** Instruction, teaching or a fee charged for educational instruction especially at a formal institution of learning. Tuition is charged by educational institutions to assist with funding of staff and faculty, course offerings, lab equipment, computer systems, libraries, facility upkeeping, and to provide a comfortable learning experience for its students.

U

- **Understanding:** A psychological process related to an abstract or physical object, such as, person, situation and message whereby one is able to think about it and use concepts to deal adequately with that object.

- **Universal preschool:** The notion that access to preschool should be available to families similar to Kindergarten. Child advocates have different definitions of the definition of who is included and how it is to be funded. There has been a move to change the name to Preschool for All.

V

- **Virtual learning environment:** (VLE) A software system designed to facilitate teachers in the management of educational courses for their students, especially by helping teachers and learners with course administration.
- **Visual learning:** A proven teaching method in which graphic organizers, such as webs, concept maps idea maps, and slide shows are used to help students of all ages think and learn more effectively.
- **Vocational education:** Prepares learners for careers or professions that are traditionally non-academic and directly related to a specific trade, occupation or *vocation*, hence the term, in which the learner participates.

W

- **Wisdom:** The ability to make correct judgments and decisions. It is an intangible quality gained through experience some think. Yet others think it is a quality that even a child, otherwise immature, may possess independent of experience or complete knowledge.

Y

- **Youth activism:** Youth voice engaged in community organizing for social change. Around the world young people are engaged as activism planners, researchers, teachers, evaluators, decision-makers, advocates and leading actors in the environmental movement, social justice organizations, and anti-racism and anti-homophobia campaigns.

Index